JESUS CHRIST
IN THE BOOK OF MORMON

OTHER COVENANT BOOKS AND AUDIO BOOKS
BY SUSAN EASTON BLACK:

400 Questions and Answers about the Book of Mormon
400 Questions and Answers about the Old Testament
400 Questions and Answers about the
Life and Times of Jesus Christ
400 Questions and Answers about the Doctrine and Covenants
Women of Character
Men of Character
Glorious Truths about Mother Eve
Glorious Truths about Mary, Mother of Jesus

JESUS CHRIST
IN THE BOOK OF MORMON

SUSAN EASTON BLACK

Covenant Communications, Inc.

Cover image: *Refuge* © Mandy Jane Williams. For more information visit www.altusfineart.com.

Cover design by Christina Marcano © 2019 by Covenant Communications, Inc.

Published by Covenant Communications, Inc.
American Fork, Utah

Copyright © 2019 by Susan Easton Black
All rights reserved. No part of this book may be reproduced in any format or in any medium without the written permission of the publisher, Covenant Communications, Inc., 1226 South 630 East, Suite 4, American Fork, UT 84003. This work is not an official publication of The Church of Jesus Christ of Latter-day Saints. The views expressed within this work are the sole responsibility of the author and do not necessarily reflect the position of The Church of Jesus Christ of Latter-day Saints, Covenant Communications, Inc., or any other entity.

Printed in the United States of America
First Printing: October 2019

25 24 23 22 21 20 19   10 9 8 7 6 5 4 3 2 1

ISBN: 978-1-52441-141-1

Dedicated to my family—
my greatest joy

TABLE OF CONTENTS

Introduction 1

Chapter One: A Fragile Testimony of Jesus Christ 3

Chapter Two: A Powerful Witness of Jesus Christ 11

Chapter Three: Christ Is at the Center of the Book of Mormon ... 17

Chapter Four: Jesus Christ Reveals Himself as a Man 25

Chapter Five: The Lord Reveals Himself as the Eternal Judge 31

Chapter Six: Central Message of Christ 39

Chapter Seven: A Personal Witness of Christ 49

Chapter Eight: His Three-Day Ministry 57

Chapter Nine: Miracles and the Believers 65

Chapter Ten: A Type and Shadow of Ancient Prophets 73

Chapter Eleven: A Testimony to Share 79

INTRODUCTION

When President Russell M. Nelson invited the sisters of the Church to read the Book of Mormon at the general women's session of the October 2018 general conference, he instructed, "As you read, I would encourage you to mark each verse that speaks of or refers to the Savior." I had read the Book of Mormon doing just that years before and knew the blessings that come from marking the verses that refer to Christ. I wrote *Finding Christ in the Book of Mormon* in 1987 for the purpose of sharing insights and miraculous changes that had occurred in my life because of reading the Book of Mormon in search of the names of Jesus Christ.

Believing that my findings are still relevant today and could help others draw closer to the Savior, I contacted Covenant Communications and asked Kathy Jenkins if this might be a publication they would consider. With a tentative "green light," I went to work.

What I had written in 1987 was still viable, but there was so much more to consider, especially as I accepted President Nelson's challenge and again read the Book of Mormon in search of Christ. The process of pulling together new facts while not discarding relevant facts discovered years ago has proven to be a labor of love. I am so appreciative of my research assistants, Deanna Durrant and Anna Arts, for sharing with me their time, talents, and insights into their own discovery of Christ in the Book of Mormon.

To my readers, I express my confidence that within these pages you will discover truths about Christ and the Book of Mormon that will brighten your day. It won't be long before you are talking with family and friends about your discoveries and "rejoicing in Christ." The bottom line—as President Nelson promised—is that you will be "drawn closer to the Savior" and experience "changes, even miracles," in your life.[1]

---

[1] Russell M. Nelson, "Sisters' Participation in the Gathering of Israel," *Ensign*, November 2018.

CHAPTER ONE
A FRAGILE TESTIMONY OF JESUS CHRIST

*When ye shall read these things,
if it be wisdom in God that ye should read them . . .
(Moroni 10:3)*

WHEN I WAS TEN YEARS old, truly memorable adventures in the classroom were rare. Any dramatic variety in the daily routine of the school doldrums was a fresh breeze to me. That is why I anticipated what was referred to in the Long Beach School District as "religious released time": two weeks in which fifth- and sixth-grade students didn't attend school. Instead they attended a local church to study religion.

Excitedly I took home the note that informed my parents of my opportunity to be a part of "released time." When my father read the note and realized that my options were to attend either the St. Barnabas Catholic Church, a Jewish synagogue, or a nondenominational worship service, he utterly refused to give his consent. It wasn't that my father was a stubborn man; it was that The Church of Jesus Christ of Latter-day Saints was his foundation, and any possible threat to his or his daughter's testimony was stopped at the front door. I tried to console myself with his answer, but for two weeks while my friends attended released time, I attended fifth grade alone. Can you imagine how boring even recess was? I vowed to be with my friends the next year, no matter what.

Running errands at home, clearing off the table, and cleaning my room all had the qualifying string attached: "Now will you let me attend 'religious released time'?" Month after month I reminded my father of the personal disaster school had been for me without my friends. I improved my grades and was kinder to my younger brother, but to no avail. The night before "released time" was to occur in sixth grade, I cried and begged my father to reconsider his decision.

My father gave in but had a few qualifiers that I had to strictly obey. I was to carry a large-sized Book of Mormon at all times and wear my Primary bandalo made of green felt each day. In retrospect, I can only suppose my father assumed that with the bandalo hanging from my neck and a Book of Mormon held in my arms, I was fully clad in the armor of God and ready for any and all attacks to my testimony.

I ran to school that day. When I met up with friends on the playground, their first question was, "Can you come?" Their second question was, "What is that green thing around your neck?" I assured them that I was coming—and that the bandalo was "a Mormon thing."

The attack on my fragile testimony came the first day from the minister of the nondenominational church. As he began to speak to the assembled children, he announced that he would be talking about God, Christ, and the Holy Ghost. He explained to us, "The Godhead is three in one, and one in three." Though perplexed by his statement, I listened intently to his explanation so that I could better understand his message. His explanation did not define three in one or one in three but instead described where God lives. "Children, God is in a cloud."

I knew that God had a body, and so in my childish mind I began to see his body stretched until it was as large as a cloud. The Lord appeared huge to me.

With this image in my mind, I heard the minister say, "Children, God is in a tree."

I imagined this very large being now becoming elongated so that he could dwell in the trunk of a tree.

The minister further stated, "Children, God is in a flower."

In my mind, the Lord had suddenly shrunk. He was very tiny.

I raised my hand, but the minister did not look at me. Instead, he droned on with a myriad of inconsistencies. To get his attention, I waved my hand back and forth. Again, I went unnoticed.

"Children, God is in a raindrop," the minister said.

In my mind I saw rain dripping and said to myself, "Are you in this drop? Or in this one? Or in that?"

I could stand the minister's message no longer. I jumped to my feet and yelled, "Stop!"

The minister stopped. The boys and girls who had been whispering and passing notes stopped. The PTA mothers who were chaperoning us stopped reprimanding my friends. Everyone stopped and stared.

"What's wrong, little girl?" the minister asked.

"What you have just said is not true!" I said.

"What is not true?"

I said boldly, "God does not live in a cloud, a tree trunk, a flower, or a raindrop. That is because God has a body just like mine and yours."

Visibly upset, the minister asked, "How do you know that?"

I quickly looked at my bandalo, hoping it would give me a clue about where I had gotten my knowledge, but it did not. I then looked at the book I was carrying. I held up my large Book of Mormon and said, "It says so in this book."

"Oh, that," replied the minister.

Dismissing the remainder of the opening devotional, he invited the other children to attend religious workshop classes. He invited me to come immediately to his office.

My friends gathered around me to assure me I was in trouble. It wasn't that I had never been to the principal's office before, but I had never been to a minister's office.

It was no small circle of friends that pointed the way to his office, but I entered alone. The minister inquired about my bandalo, but he was definitely more interested in my book.

"Where in that book does it say God has a body?" he asked.

I flipped through several pages quickly, hoping to open to just the right verse.

He then exclaimed, "You appear to be having difficulty locating what you are seeking. Could it be that you have never read the Book of Mormon?"

I admitted, "I have never read this book."

Angered by my outburst in the chapel and now my ignorance as to my knowledge of God, he opened the door of his office and invited a PTA mother to escort me back to school.

For the next two weeks I read the Book of Mormon while my friends attended "religious released time." Even during recess, I continued to read. I cannot, in all honesty, say that during my first reading of the Book of Mormon I had an experience similar to that of Mary Elizabeth Rollins, who begged to read the book. Mary wrote, "I felt such a desire to read it, that I could not refrain from asking [Isaac Morley] to let me take it home and read it, while he attended meeting."[2]

Nor was my experience equal to Parley P. Pratt's first reading of the book. Parley stated: "I read all day; eating was a burden, I had no desire

---

[2] Lavina Fielding Anderson, "Kirtland's Resolute Saints," *Ensign*, January 1979; N. B. Lundwall, *The Life and Testimony of Mary E. Lightner*, n.p., n.d. Church History Library, Salt Lake City.

for food; sleep was a burden when the night came, I preferred reading to sleep. As I read, the spirit of the Lord was upon me, and I knew and comprehended that the book was true, as plainly and manifestly as a man comprehends and knows that he exists. My joy was now full."[3]

Yet I *can* say that I read. I was looking intently for just the right answer to the question the minister had posed, "Where in that book does it say God has a body?"

I was disappointed, as I began my search, not to find the answer in the first verse of 1 Nephi. As I read on, I learned about travels in the wilderness, broken bows, dreams, wickedness, and warfare—but where was my answer? I struggled through the Isaiah chapters, but again found no answer. As I read on, I discovered that the Book of Mormon contained many messages, yet my first reading of it left me in a quandary. Where was the answer I was seeking? I did not find it.

On reflection, I now view that first experience with the Book of Mormon as comparable to that of a hurried tourist who exclaims, "Yes, I have been there. I saw the monuments, but I didn't get to know the people." In that first reading, it was as though I said, "Of course I read the Book of Mormon, but I didn't find the nature of God."

Did my testimony hinge on whether the Book of Mormon was true or The Church of Jesus Christ of Latter-day Saints was the Lord's true church upon the earth? Not in the least. The ward meetinghouse was a place to see my friends, catch up on their news, and make plans for the week. Church was an integral part of my life, as well as that of my brothers' and my parents' lives. My father golfed with his Church friends during the week, my mother spent hours on the phone talking to her Relief Society friends, and I looked for Church friends at school.

If someone had asked me whether Joseph Smith used the Urim and Thummin or a stone in a hat to translate the Book of Mormon, I would have had no opinion and would not have cared about the answer. The same went for theories about the authorship of the Book of Mormon and whether Joseph Smith was a dreamer and concocted the words himself or was the translator. All I knew was that my family went to church every week and we were happy.

As I grew into teenage years, I questioned the rules in my family but not whether The Church of Jesus Christ of Latter-day Saints had the truth. I didn't equate curfew and not swimming on Sunday with the

---

[3] *Autobiography of Parley Parker Pratt, One of the Twelve Apostles of The Church of Jesus Christ of Latter-day Saints*, ed. Parley P. Pratt Jr. (Chicago: Law, King, and Law, 1888), 38.

Church. I saw it as my parents' heavy hand—their rules. It was not until mu young adult years, when I was asked to give significant time in service to the Church, that questions arose. Initially, they had more to do with personality conflicts in the ward than doctrine. But as the years passed, simple questions about doctrine that began with *Why?* took center stage. Rather than pepper the gospel doctrine teacher with questions that may or may not have had an answer, I purchased a journal and filled it with my queries.

Was Joseph Smith reading from the Bible when he dictated the Isaiah portion of the Book of Mormon? Why did Nephi write that Jesus was born in Jerusalem? How many times did angel Moroni visit Joseph Smith? Did Joseph Smith see Mormon, Nephi, and the disciples called by Jesus in the land of Bountiful? How much of the Book of Mormon did Emma Smith scribe? Could portions of the Book of Lehi be reconstructed from what is contained in the small plates?

Finding the answers to these questions and a host of others became a treasure hunt for me. It was never a quest to know if the Book of Mormon was true (that was a given); it was always to fill in the blanks and gain greater knowledge. More than once, I wished that angel Moroni had given Joseph Smith an addendum. In the quiet of my home, I read the works of Book of Mormon scholars Hugh Nibley and George Reynolds, never dreaming that such reading was preparatory for the day I would be teaching Book of Mormon classes at Brigham Young University. I saw the hunt as a hobby—nothing more.

A week before I taught my first Book of Mormon class at the university, I made an appointment to meet with scholar Robert J. Matthews, chair of Ancient Scripture. For the meeting, I had prepared a five-page, single-spaced document listing the books and articles I had read about the Book of Mormon. I handed the document to Brother Matthews and asked him to look it over. He gave it a cursory glance as I assured him that I had made notes on each entry and had memorized my notes. The comment was not to impress Brother Matthews but to prepare him for my question: "Have I missed reading anything written about the Book of Mormon?" Brother Matthews now carefully looked over my list before saying, "Yes! I don't see anywhere that you have read the Book of Mormon."

"Since childhood I have read and reread the book many times," I assured him.

"I know that, Susan," Brother Matthews said. "This time I want you to read it and find the nature of the Godhead, but first I want you to find Jesus Christ. I want you to find him in each chapter. I want you to return to my office with a testimony that the entire Book of Mormon is another witness for Jesus Christ."

I left Brother Matthews' office muttering to myself, *Find Christ in each chapter? How is that possible? The Book of Mormon is about civilizations that failed—Nephites, Jaredites, Lamanites, and Zoramites. You name it, civilizations fail.*

That night, feeling very discouraged and alone, I opened the Book of Mormon and read the title page. One phrase caught my attention. I read it over and over. Could Robert J. Matthews be right? Was this *entire* book about Christ? The phrase announced plainly and directly that the purpose of the book was "the convincing of the Jew and Gentile that JESUS is the CHRIST" (Title Page). If that was the purpose, then I had quite overlooked the book's recurrent, most powerful, most timely message. I had seen the surface—the broken bow and the voyage to the promised land—but had missed the heart of the book.

That night and subsequent nights changed my life. I now know from years of diligent and prayerful searching that the Book of Mormon has been preserved to come forth in these latter days to convince me and the "Jew and Gentile that JESUS is the CHRIST, the ETERNAL GOD" (Title Page). Its purpose is to verify with thousands of references the divine Sonship of Jesus to those who "ask with a sincere heart, with real intent, having faith in Christ" (Moroni 10:4). I concur with Elder Bruce R. McConkie, who proclaimed, "If ever there was a compilation of inspired writings that stand as a witness of the divine Sonship of the Lord Jesus Christ, that work is the Book of Mormon!"[4]

When President Russell M. Nelson invited the sisters of the Church to read the Book of Mormon at the general women's session of the October 2018 general conference, he promised that "the heavens will open for you. The Lord will bless you with increased inspiration and revelation." He then instructed, "As you read, I would encourage you to mark each verse that speaks of or refers to the Savior. Then, be intentional about talking of Christ, rejoicing in Christ, and preaching of Christ with your families and friends. You and they will be drawn closer to the Savior through this process." He assured the sisters that by so doing "changes, even miracles, will begin to happen."[5]

---

[4] Bruce R. McConkie, *The Promised Messiah: The First Coming of Christ* (Salt Lake City: Deseret Book, 1978), 145.
[5] Nelson, "Sisters' Participation in the Gathering of Israel."

As one who has followed that process of finding Christ in the Book of Mormon, I know that President Nelson is right. I want to share with you the answers I have found. The words I write are born of years of prayerful searching that began so long ago. I hope they convey to you the adventure of my quest, my unexpected discoveries along the way, and my subsequent joy in the knowledge that the Book of Mormon is indeed a powerful witness of Jesus Christ, our Savior and Redeemer. My hope is that these glimpses into eternal realms will benefit you in your search to know more about our Savior. I hope that one of my readers is a minister in Long Beach. I would like to apologize to him for my youthful outburst but not my answer: "It says so in this book."

CHAPTER TWO
A POWERFUL WITNESS OF JESUS CHRIST

*When ye shall read these things . . .
remember how merciful the Lord hath been.
(Moroni 10:3)*

IT TOOK ME NEARLY A lifetime to discover that the central message of the Book of Mormon is Jesus Christ. For too many years, I was satisfied with reading about a family voyage to the promised land and of their descendants struggling to hold on to the iron rod. During these years, my testimony of the Book of Mormon was fragile but not easily swayed.

Critics who dismissed the Book of Mormon as nothing more than a hoax, a fraud, or an evidence of Joseph Smith's imagination and cunning held little interest for me. The reason for my disinterest had everything to do their condemnation of holy scripture on the basis of purported research, exclusive information, and assumed expertise that was riddled with intellectual caverns. How they continue to rationalize that Joseph Smith read from a manuscript written by Solomon Spaulding, or that Sidney Rigdon wrote the Book of Mormon is beyond my understanding when so much evidence is piled up against such claims. Yet that doesn't stop critics from churning out flawed propaganda for the internet, hoping to ensnare the elect. The critics must lament that they only entrap the ill-informed by hurling gratuitous verbiage at the word of God. Such demeaning actions cause *them*, not the Book of Mormon, to appear foolish. And not so surprising, the critics never discover that the Book of Mormon is centered on Christ.

This last comment could also be said of hobbyists and "would-be" archaeologists, whose interest in external evidence suggests their purpose in perusing the Book of Mormon is to explore hypotheses centered on the possible location of the land of Nephi and archaeological artifacts that date back to antiquity. Discoveries of complex monetary systems in pre-Columbian America (see Alma 11:4–19), cement (see Helaman 3:7, 9, 11), copper (see 1 Nephi 18:25; 2 Nephi 5:15), sophisticated tools (see 1 Nephi 17:9; Jarom 1:8; Ether 10:25–26), machinery (see Jarom 1:8), and excellent highways (see 3 Nephi 6:8) certainly support prophetic claims, as do scholarly evidences of advanced civilizations, fluctuations in economic growth, trends in migration, and devastations of war. Museums throughout North and South America support much of the historical references of the Book of Mormon and bolster reasons for archeologists' and hobbyists' hypotheses. But as interesting and applicable as these findings are with the cultural details of the Book of Mormon, they pale in comparison to the revealed Christ found within the pages of the Book of Mormon.

Then there are the comparative Latter-day Saint anthropologists who focus on Old World culture and worship. Too often, they see the Book of Mormon as a point of reference for comparing and contrasting Eastern and Western civilizations. After all, both cultures wrote on plates of metal (see 1 Nephi 4:16), viewed oaths as binding (see 1 Nephi 4:33, 35, 37), held sacred the law of Moses (using burnt offerings in worship—see 1 Nephi 5:9; 7:22; Mosiah 2:3), intermixed idol worship in their culture (see Helaman 6:31; Alma 17:15; Alma 31:1), and had people who sacrificed to idols (see Mormon 4:14, 21) and built altars of stones (see 1 Nephi 2:7). These similarities, along with curious but explainable differences, are intellectually stimulating and often the subject of papers presented at Book of Mormon symposiums but are not necessarily spiritually edifying. Such scholarship, although detailed and specific, is an aside, for it misses the Christ-centered purpose of the Book of Mormon.

Then there are the readers who find Christ in Third Nephi and compare and contrast the visit of the resurrected Lord with ancient legends of a white god. There is more than one account of a white god visiting the inhabitants of the western hemisphere. The people of Mexico call their white, bearded god Quetzalcoatl; the Polynesian cultures call their god Wakea; the primitive tribes on the upper Amazon River in South America refer to him as Wako; and the natives in the Andean Region call him Viracocha. The legends of a white god descending to earth strengthens the idea of an actual visit of Deity to America but lacks the convincing evidence found in the Book of Mormon.

Those who read the Book of Mormon without a Christ-centered focus will find a history of people who inhabited the Western hemisphere from about 600 BC to AD 421. As the pages of the text unfold, readers learn of civilizations plagued by evil men and women: robbers (see Helaman 2), anti-Christs (see Alma 30), and seductresses (see Alma 39). They learn of treachery (see Alma 47), wars (see Alma 43; Helaman 4), defense tactics (see Alma 43), and prison walls (see Helaman 5:27). By contrast, they also learn of courageous kings (see Mosiah 2:27), of integrity (see Mosiah 11–17), and of faithfulness (see Alma 32). They find the plot of the Book of Mormon filled with high adventure as the great contest between the forces of good and evil combine to present a vibrant, intriguing history of a people oscillating between grandeur and destruction. Yet, by focusing on the oscillating civilizations, it is too easy to miss the purpose of the Book of Mormon: it is "Another Testament of Jesus Christ."

Try reading the Book of Mormon whie searching for Christ as the central theme on every page. A simple request, but when you do it, the words of God will fill your soul with that spirit that has inspired thousands of faithful Latter-day Saints to accept mission calls and spend millions of dollars to travel the globe to share the Book of Mormon. I myself have served as one of the missionaries in the United States, in Chile, and on Easter Island. Certainly, I did not labor to share a book of high adventure, a treatise on archaeological ruins, a manuscript on the origin of the Native Americans, or a comparative study of ancient American legends. I believe the same could be said for all missionaries of The Church of Jesus Christ of Latter-day Saints who now labor throughout the world. After all, would people in Germany, South Africa, Korea, England, or Australia express interest in hearing about such a text, let alone read it, if mere historical fact, American archeology, or comparative studies were its purpose?

Is it conceivable that a mere history of a thousand years translated in the 1820s would still be in print today? Certainly not! But did you know that by January 2019, the Book of Mormon was not only still in print in the English language but translated into ninety languages, and portions of the book have been translated into twenty-one other languages? A conservative count from 1830 to 1981 shows there were 27,249,193 copies of the book distributed. Since then, the count has increased exponentially. In the year 2017 alone, there were 4,804,282 copies of the Book of Mormon distributed. By January 2019, the rough estimate is that 186 million copies of the Book of Mormon have been distributed.[6] Such published numbers would be impossible if the book were merely a historical account of people who lived in ancient America.

---

[6] Rick Crowther, telephone conversation, January 2019.

What is the reason for the compelling worldwide demand for the Book of Mormon? The answer is simple: the Book of Mormon reveals Christ.

In our fast-paced, twenty-first century lives, most people who are looking at their devices, waiting for the next incoming text, would not be inclined to read a double-columned book of more than five hundred pages if it were presented merely as something of interest to the scholar, the curious, or the well-meaning. If you were to recognize, however, that through pondering the message of the Book of Mormon you could comprehend, as you could in no other way, the nature of our Father in Heaven, His Son Jesus the Christ, and the Holy Ghost, you would understand why so many people read the Book of Mormon with intensity on a daily basis.

Unfortunately, even these readers settle for something far less than finding Christ in the Book of Mormon. Failing to find the key, they fail to recognize the reason that has moved missionaries, pioneers, and today's Latter-day Saints to devote all to the quest. In case you are wondering, the bottom line is this: the Book of Mormon is a rich and powerful witness of Jesus Christ. The book witnesses not only that He is, but also who He is, how He thinks, how He feels, and how He acts. By reading the book looking for references to Christ, you enter into its holy inner meaning instead of just admiring the surrounding courtyards. You come to truly know of Jesus Christ through the catalytic words of Book of Mormon prophets, for their central purpose was to reveal Him to you.

For example, beginning with chapter 1 of First Nephi, the first chapter of the Book of Mormon, you will learn that:

1. The Lord highly favored Nephi in all his days (see 1 Nephi 1:1). You might wonder if the Lord has favorites today. Could you be one of His favorites?
2. Knowledge of the goodness and mysteries of God is available to you (see 1 Nephi 1:1).
3. The way to speak to the Lord is through prayer (see 1 Nephi 1:5).
4. You can receive heavenly manifestations while praying to the Lord with all your heart (see 1 Nephi 1:6).
5. God can be seen in vision sitting on a throne surrounded by angels singing and praising Him (see 1 Nephi 1:8).
6. The Lord can show future events to you (see 1 Nephi 1:9–13, 15).

7. You can be filled with the Spirit of the Lord (see 1 Nephi 1:12).
8. The correct response to a heavenly manifestation is to praise God: "Great and marvelous are thy works, O Lord God Almighty!" (1 Nephi 1:14).
9. The Messiah will come to redeem the world (see 1 Nephi 1:19).
10. The Lord is merciful to "those whom he hath chosen, because of their faith, to make them mighty even unto the power of deliverance" (see 1 Nephi 1:20).

The information available to those who truly wish to know and to be like Christ far supersedes in importance the almost irrelevant but prevalent discussions of whether Nephi's bow was made of pure steel or a combination of wood and steel (see 1 Nephi 16:18), why Lehi wanted Lemuel to be firm and steadfast as a valley instead of firm and steadfast as a mountain or a rock (see 1 Nephi 2:10), or whether Noah's ark was shaped like the Jaredite barges (see Ether 6:7). Answers to these questions might add some context to the text, but they do not lead directly to the central message, the convincing assurance that "JESUS is the CHRIST, the ETERNAL GOD" (Title Page).

If you seek to know, you will find that the Book of Mormon writers wrote primarily about our Savior. They wrote of Him because of their conviction of His divinity, for they knew of Him and loved Him: "For, for this intent have we written these things, that they may know that we knew of Christ, and we had a hope of his glory many hundred years before his coming; and not only we ourselves had a hope of his glory, but also all the holy prophets which were before us" (Jacob 4:4).

The writers did not gain this knowledge by comparing the customs, characteristics, lifestyles, and mannerisms of Lehi's family with families living around the land of Jerusalem in 600 BC, nor did they gain knowledge of Jesus through findings unearthed by archaeologists, such as skeletal remains, gold plates, cement highways, and places of worship in the ancient Americas. Neither did they grasp a knowledge of the Messiah through acquaintance with Native American traditions, folklore, or legends of voyages and wars. The Holy One was revealed to the ancient prophets of the Book of Mormon by the power of the Holy Ghost.

By the power of the Holy Ghost, prophets wrote a witness for Jesus Christ—the Book of Mormon—and by that same power, the ancient prophets knew that their writings would bear testimony to you that Jesus is the Christ.

If you do not seek to find Christ in the Book of Mormon, you can almost completely miss a testimony of the book. If you do seek to find Christ, He reverberates, dominates, and thunders on every page, in every chapter, and in every verse.

At the October 2017 general conference, Elder Tad R. Callister said, "One of my good and bright friends left the Church for a time." Elder Callister then said of his friend, "He recently wrote to me of his return." The return had everything to do with how he read the Book of Mormon:

> Initially, I wanted the Book of Mormon to be proven to me historically, geographically, linguistically, and culturally. But when I changed my focus to what it teaches about the gospel of Jesus Christ and His saving mission, I began to gain a testimony of its truthfulness. One day while reading the Book of Mormon in my room, I paused, knelt down, and gave a heartfelt prayer and felt resoundingly that Heavenly Father whispered to my spirit that the Church and the Book of Mormon were definitely true. My three-and-a-half-year period of reinvestigating the Church led me back wholeheartedly and convincingly to its truthfulness."[7]

To the prayerful, sincere, and questioning, I want to make it clear—I know the Book of Mormon will bear a powerful testimony to you that "JESUS is the CHRIST, the ETERNAL GOD" (Title Page). The reason for my confidence is because "the book itself is a new witness for Christ. From first to last it bears record that he is the Son of God and teaches in plainness and perfection the truths of his everlasting gospel."[8]

To the critic, however, the Book of Mormon will remain a figment of Joseph Smith's imagination. To the friendly scholar it will continue to be a reference point. To the curious it is one more interesting legend. To the well-meaning it is only a history filled with examples of good and bad behavior. But to the seeker after truth and righteousness, the Book of Mormon is a revelation of who God is and stands with the Old and New Testaments as a witness that "JESUS is the CHRIST, the ETERNAL GOD" (Title Page).

---

[7] Elder Tad R. Callister, "God's Compelling Witness: The Book of Mormon," *Ensign*, November 2017.

[8] McConkie, *The Promised Messiah*, 297.

CHAPTER THREE
CHRIST IS AT THE CENTER OF THE BOOK OF MORMON

We talk of Christ, we rejoice in Christ, we preach of Christ, we prophesy of Christ, and we write according to our prophecies . . .
(2 Nephi 25:26)

As an associate dean of General Education and Honors at Brigham Young University, it was my privilege to invite professors to present a lecture to the honors students at a morning devotional each week. Hoping that the professors would deliver a lecture on a topic that was meaningful to them and the students, I suggested that they consider the topic, "My Last Lecture." In other words, I invited them to speak as if they were presenting their final lecture. I hoped the professors would speak passionately about the most important subject of their scholarly career, or what Alma called "the wish of mine heart" (Alma 29:1).

When I was given the same opportunity, I spoke of what is written in this chapter, for it was and continues to be "the wish of mine heart" (Alma 29:1). It is my greatest discovery as a professor.

Books	References to Christ	Verses	Average
First Nephi	474	618	1.303
Second Nephi	591	779	1.318
Jacob	156	203	1.301
Enos	22	27	1.227
Jarom	8	15	1.875
Omni	20	30	1.500
Words of Mormon	15	18	1.200

Books	References to Christ	Verses	Average
Mosiah	492	785	1.596
Alma	1,013	1,975	1.950
Helaman	225	497	2.209
Third Nephi	293	788	2.589
Fourth Nephi	42	49	1.167
Mormon	188	227	1.207
Ether	220	433	1.968
Moroni	166	163	1.108
TOTAL	3,927	6,607	1.682

I discovered through the above figures that the Book of Mormon prophets mentioned some form of Christ's name on an average of once every 1.7 verses. By comparison, the New Testament writers mentioned a form of His name on an average of once every 2.1 verses.[9] Thus, the name of the Savior appears nearly 24 percent more frequently in the Book of Mormon than in the New Testament.

When you realize that a verse usually consists of one sentence, you cannot, on the average, read two sentences in the Book of Mormon without seeing some form of Christ's name.

These references to Christ are not distributed without appropriate relationship to the text. For instance, fewer references to Christ are made during periods of darkness, apostasy, and war, probably because His influence is lessened by the unrighteous actions of the people (see, for example, Alma 50–59). During periods of peace, joy, and prosperity, which come when the ancient people kept the commandments, names for Jesus Christ are used profusely because circumstances indicate the abundant presence of His Spirit (see, for example, 4 Nephi).

Although His name appears often throughout the Book of Mormon, it does not appear as monotonous or chanting repetition. Each appearance of the Savior's name reveals something unique, something essential, and something deeply inspirational about Him. By tallying how many different names there are for Christ, you will discover that the prophetic scribes of the Book of Mormon referred to Jesus Christ by literally 101 different names. They are shown below, listed alphabetically:

---

[9] Lee A. Crandall, "New Testament Study on the Use of the Names of Deity," n. p.

Names/Titles for Jesus Christ in the Book of Mormon

Almighty	2 Nephi 23:6
Almighty God	Jacob 2:10
Alpha and Omega	3 Nephi 9:18
Being	Mosiah 4:19
Beloved	2 Nephi 31:15
Beloved Son	2 Nephi 31:11
Christ	2 Nephi 10:3
Christ Jesus	Alma 5:44
Christ the Son	Alma 11:44
Counselor	2 Nephi 19:6
Creator	2 Nephi 9:5
Eternal Father	Mosiah 15:4
Eternal God	1 Nephi 12:18
Eternal Head	Helaman 13:38
Eternal Judge	Moroni 10:34
Everlasting Father	2 Nephi 19:6
Everlasting God	1 Nephi 15:15
Father	Jacob 7:22
Father of Heaven	1 Nephi 22:9
Father of Heaven and of Earth	Helaman 14:12
Founder of Peace	Mosiah 15:18
God	2 Nephi 1:22
God of Abraham	1 Nephi 19:10
God of Abraham, Isaac, and Jacob	Mosiah 7:19
God of Abraham, and of Isaac, and the God of Jacob	1 Nephi 19:10
God of Isaac	Alma 29:11
God of Israel	1 Nephi 19:7
God of Jacob	2 Nephi 12:3
God of Miracles	2 Nephi 27:23

God of Nature	1 Nephi 19:12
God of the Whole Earth	3 Nephi 11:14
Good Shepherd	Alma 5:38
Great Creator	2 Nephi 9:5
Great Spirit	Alma 18:2
Head	Jacob 4:17
Holy Child	Moroni 8:3
Holy God	2 Nephi 9:39
Holy Messiah	2 Nephi 2:6
Holy One	2 Nephi 2:10
Holy One of Israel	1 Nephi 19:14
Holy One of Jacob	2 Nephi 27:34
Husband	3 Nephi 22:5
Immanuel	2 Nephi 18:8
Jehovah	Moroni 10:34
Jesus	2 Nephi 31:10
Jesus Christ	2 Nephi 25:19
Keeper of the Gate	2 Nephi 9:41
King	2 Nephi 16:5
King of Heaven	2 Nephi 10:14
Lamb	1 Nephi 13:35
Lamb of God	1 Nephi 10:10
Lord	1 Nephi 10:14
Lord God	2 Nephi 1:5
Lord God Almighty	2 Nephi 9:46
Lord God Omnipotent	Mosiah 3:21
Lord God of Hosts	2 Nephi 13:15
Lord Jehovah	2 Nephi 22:2
Lord Jesus	Moroni 6:6
Lord Jesus Christ	Mosiah 3:12
Lord of Hosts	1 Nephi 20:2

Lord of the Vineyard	Jacob 5:8
Lord Omnipotent	Mosiah 3:5
Maker	2 Nephi 9:40
Man	3 Nephi 11:8
Master	Jacob 5:4
Mediator	2 Nephi 2:28
Messiah	1 Nephi 1:19
Mighty God	2 Nephi 6:17
Mighty One of Israel	1 Nephi 22:12
Mighty One of Jacob	1 Nephi 21:26
Most High	2 Nephi 24:14
Most High God	Alma 26:14
Only Begotten of the Father	2 Nephi 25:12
Only Begotten Son	Jacob 4:5
Prince of Peace	2 Nephi 19:6
Prophet	1 Nephi 22:20
Rabbanah	Alma 18:13
Redeemer	1 Nephi 10:6
Redeemer of Israel	1 Nephi 21:7
Redeemer of the World	1 Nephi 10:5
Rock	1 Nephi 15:15
Savior	2 Nephi 31:13
Savior Jesus Christ	3 Nephi 5:20
Savior of the World	1 Nephi 10:4
Shepherd	1 Nephi 13:41
Son	2 Nephi 31:13
Son of God	1 Nephi 10:17
Son of Righteousness	Ether 9:22
Son of the Eternal Father	1 Nephi 11:21
Son of the Everlasting God	1 Nephi 11:32
Son of the Living God	2 Nephi 31:16

Son of the Most High God	1 Nephi 11:6
Stone	Jacob 4:16
Supreme Being	Alma 11:22
Supreme Creator	Alma 30:44
True and Living God	1 Nephi 17:30
True Messiah	2 Nephi 1:10
True Shepherd	Helaman 15:13
True Vine	1 Nephi 15:15
Well Beloved	Helaman 5:47
Wonderful	2 Nephi 19:6

Each of the 101 names signified to the prophetic writers a different attribute or characteristic of Jesus Christ, and each name was used to convey recognition of who He is and what His mission represents. For example, Lord Omnipotent means that Christ is the Lord of all, possessing all power. Holy One signifies that He is holy and without sin, being perfect in all things. God of the Whole Earth reflects His universal interest in all people and in their individual redemption. And Savior means that Jesus came to save His people from their sins.

Each title signifying Christ is presented in correct contextual usage each time it appears. For example, when the subject of the scriptural verse is the Atonement, the title Redeemer is used to designate our Savior, not the title Holy Child or True Vine.

The names given to our Lord take on new significance when you approach them through a thoughtful and a sensitive study of their meaning. His character, mission, and divine relationship to you is thereby more clearly revealed. Each verse in which His name appears is given enriched meaning because of the definition of Christ's name.

The following is a partial list of names/titles for Christ and their meaning:

Almighty God. This title signifies a holy being having all power and unlimited might.

Alpha and Omega. These words, being the first and last letters of the Greek alphabet, are used figuratively to teach the timelessness and eternal nature of our Lord's existence.

Beloved Son. This title signifies Christ's favored, preferential, chosen, and beloved status as well as His divine Sonship.

Counselor. The name bears record of His preeminent position among men where the exercise of deliberate judgment and prudence is concerned.

Creator. The creative work of this world and other worlds without number is done by Christ as directed by the Father.

Eternal God. This name signifies that God is from everlasting to everlasting, beyond finite comprehension in power, dominion, godly attributes, and eternal glory.

God of Israel. This title signifies His personal, attentive care of the Israelites.

God of Nature. Through Christ's almighty power, all things in nature are created, upheld, governed, and controlled.

Good Shepherd. His Saints are the sheep, His sheepfold is His Church, and He is the Shepherd.

Holy Messiah. This name signifies His holy and perfected state and His position as Deliverer and King

Holy One of Israel. He is both the embodiment of holiness and the God of Israel, who came into the world through the lineage of His chosen people.

Husband. Christ (the Bridegroom) shall claim His bride (the Church), celebrate the marriage supper, and become the Husband of His wife.

Immanuel. Christ as God was born into mortality of a virgin and would be with men to save and redeem them.

Jehovah. This title means God of Israel.

Jesus. This title is the masculine personal name, meaning Jehovah is salvation or deliverance.

Keeper of the Gate. He shall admit men into the presence of the Father. He opens the gate to the righteous and bars it to the wicked.

King. Christ is the Ruler, Lawgiver, and Sovereign in whom all power rests. As King, He rules over the heavens and the earth and all things that are in them.

Lamb of God. He takes away the sins of the world. As a Lamb, He was sacrificed for men. Salvation comes because of the shedding of His blood.

Lord. He is supreme in authority and sovereign over all.

Master. He stood as a teacher, ruler, and commander.

Mediator. A mediator is one who interposes himself between parties at variance to reconcile them. Christ filled this office as part of His great atoning sacrifice.

Most High. This title designates a state of supreme exaltation in rank, power, and dignity.

Only Begotten Son. Christ is the only Son of the Father in the flesh.

Prince of Peace. In the gospel of Christ are the principles that bring us peace when we obey them.

Prophet. By every test, Christ was the greatest of the prophets. He was a teacher, revealer, and witness of the truth.

Redeemer. Christ ransomed and redeemed men from the effects of the Fall of Adam.

Rock. This name carries a connotation of strength and stability.

The Mighty God. The all-powerful One, the Mighty God of Jacob.

True Vine. Christ is the True Vine, His Father is the Husbandman, His prophets are the branches, and the fruit the branches bear is eternal life for the souls of men.

Being aware of the variety of references to the Savior and having an understanding of the rich meaning of each name inspires reverential awe for our Beloved Redeemer. But the personal witness that Jesus is the Christ is achieved only through a sacred, revealed witness. You will receive the conviction that Jesus is the Christ when God, the Eternal Father, manifests the truth of it "by the power of the Holy Ghost" (Moroni 10:4). That spirit of testimony comes as you read the Book of Mormon looking for Christ. That testimony will fill your soul with joy even on the darkest of days.

What have you learned thus far? Christ is central to the Book of Mormon. There are 101 positive, divine titles for Christ, each title appearing consistently and correctly in its context. Add to this the fact that Jesus's name appears nearly four thousand times, on an average of once every 1.7 verses. Can you draw any other conclusion than that the divinity of Jesus of Nazareth is powerfully proclaimed by prophets in the Book of Mormon?

CHAPTER FOUR
JESUS CHRIST REVEALS HIMSELF AS A MAN

*They cast their eyes up again towards heaven; and behold,
they saw a Man descending out of heaven;
and he was clothed in a white robe.*
(3 Nephi 11:8)

KNOWING THE NAMES/TITLES FOR Jesus Christ and their definitions presents a real opportunity for you and me to discover more about our Savior. For example, the title Man means the Savior looks like an adult man, but there is so much more to learn.

No doubt when you think of the word *man* in a scriptural sense, Adam comes to mind. In Moses 2:26, the Lord God said, "Unto mine Only Begotten [Jesus the Christ], which was with me from the beginning: Let us make man in our image, after our likeness." According to President Gordon B. Hinckley, this moment in the Creation was the beginning of God's "crowning creation"—the climax of the six creative periods.[10] This creative period was greater than the lights in the firmament, the seas, the trees, the fowls of the air, the beasts, and "every creeping thing that creepeth upon the earth" (Genesis 1:22, 26). Yet all these needed to be in place before the formation of man—"an event of such transcendent import . . . that neither heaven nor earth are ever thereafter the same."[11]

The creation of man was not a response to a divine utterance like "let the waters bring forth abundantly the moving creature that hath life" (Genesis 1:20), it required direct involvement of God the Father and His Son Jesus Christ. "So the Gods went down to organize man

---
[10] Gordon B. Hinckley, "The Women in Our Lives," *Ensign*, November 2004.
[11] Bruce R. McConkie, "Once or Twice in a Thousand Years," *Ensign*, November 1975.

in their own image, in the image of the Gods to form they him," said President Russell M. Nelson, quoting Abraham 4:7.[12] "And the Lord God formed man of the dust of the ground, and breathed into his nostrils the breath of life; and man became a living soul" (Genesis 2:7; see also Moses 3:7; Abraham 5:7).

But what of His Creator and the title *Man* for Jesus Christ? When the Lord showed Himself to the brother of Jared, He declared, "Seest thou that ye are created after mine own image? Yea, even all men were created in the beginning after mine own image" (Ether 3:15). This has been the case with man from the beginning, or as the Prophet Joseph Smith said, "If the veil were rent today, and the great God who holds this world in its orbit, and who upholds all worlds and all things by His power, was to make himself visible—I say, if you were to see him today, you would see him like a man in form—like yourselves in all the person, image, and very form as a man."[13]

The reason Jesus Christ was seen in the form of a man is because He is a man—"Man of Holiness is his name" (Moses 6:57). Moses so testified, as did a multitude near the temple in the land of Bountiful in AD 34. Although they had heard the voice of God the Father say, "Behold my Beloved Son, in whom I am well pleased, in whom I have glorified my name—hear ye him," they saw only a man like unto themselves descending to the earth (3 Nephi 11:7). They wrongfully concluded that the descending man dressed in white was an angel—not Jesus Christ, of whom the prophets had testified (see 3 Nephi 11:8). Yet, there was no question in their minds that the figure descending to the earth was a man.

To give the multitude a witness that the man standing before them was their Savior, in charitable magnitude the resurrected Lord invited the multitude to become sure witnesses of Him. They were to step forward and thrust their hands into His side and feel the prints of the nails in His hands and feet (see 3 Nephi 11:14). Notice the body parts of the man named in the scriptural passage—side, hands, and feet. They were not asked to hug Him so they could feel that He had a back or shake His hand and feel the grasp of His fingers and thumb. They were asked to thrust their hands into His side and feel the prints of the nails in His hands and feet. These are the very body parts that evidence this man bore the marks of crucifixion.

With that privilege of touch came the realization that this man was *The* Man—their Savior, their Redeemer, and their Deliverer. He was the

---

[12] Russell M. Nelson, "The Creation," *Ensign*, May 2000.

[13] Joseph Smith Jr., "The King Follett Sermon," Joseph Smith Papers.

Christ who had taken upon Himself the sins of all mortals. He was the very man prophets had testified of through the ages.

The multitude had heard God the Father introduce Him and Christ introduce Himself—"I am Jesus Christ, whom the prophets testified shall come into the world"—but it was not until they used the sense of touch that the multitude became sure witnesses of the resurrected Lord (3 Nephi 11:10). In that touch, the abridger Mormon never suggests that the man standing before them had scales, fur, horns, wings, or any other physical feature that characterizes mammals, birds, or other creatures. Mormon wrote only of the resurrected Lord looking like a man—like any other man in the multitude except for the marks of crucifixion.

A search in the Book of Mormon verifies this fact. There are 283 references to Jesus Christ having a body with parts identical to that of mortal man. This clearly shows that Christ is a man, not part of the ethereal Trinity of mainline Christianity. In most references, the body part of Christ that is mentioned is literal. In other references, the body part is figurative or part of a metaphor.

The Lord Reveals Himself as a Man

Arm	1 Nephi 20:14

Arms
    Holy Arms—Enos 1:13
    Open Arms—Mormon 6:17
	2 Nephi 1:15

Back	2 Nephi 7:6
Blood	Alma 5:21
Bowels	Mosiah 15:9
Ear	2 Nephi 7:5
Ears	2 Nephi 15:9
Eye All-Searching Eye—2 Nephi 9:44	Jacob 2:15

Eyes
    Eyes of His Glory—2 Nephi 13:8
    Piercing Eye—Jacob 2:10
	2 Nephi 3:8

Face	2 Nephi 7:6
Feet	3 Nephi 11:15

Finger	Alma 10:2
Flesh	Alma 7:12
Hand	1 Nephi 20:13
Hands	2 Nephi 1:24
Left Hand—Mosiah 5:10	
Palms of My Hands—1 Nephi 21:16	
Right Hand—1 Nephi 20:13	
Lips	2 Nephi 21:4
Loins	2 Nephi 21:5
Mouth	2 Nephi 3:21
Shoulder	2 Nephi 19:6
Side	3 Nephi 11:14
Tongue	2 Nephi 7:4

Voice
    Mighty Voice—Alma 5:51
    Mildness of the Voice—Helaman 5:31
    Pleasant Voice—Helaman 5:46
    Small Voice—3 Nephi 11:3
    Still Small Voice—1 Nephi 17:45
    Still Voice of Perfect Mildness—Helaman 5:30
    Not a Voice of a Great Tumultuous Noise—Helaman 5:30
    Voice of Thunder—1 Nephi 17:45
	1 Nephi 16:25

The Lord uses His body parts much like mortal man uses his. There is not an instance in the Book of Mormon where the Lord uses His hands to do something unusual like run or speak. The same could be said for His ears, eyes, tongue, and so forth. The Lord symbolically used His hands to guide (see 2 Nephi 1:24) and to recover His children (see 2 Nephi 21:11). He used His voice, His mouth, and His tongue to converse with His chosen people (see Helaman 5:30); to chasten them (see 1 Nephi 16:25); and to command them (see 1 Nephi 3:2). He used His mighty arms to protect (see Enos 1:13) and to receive His followers (see Mormon 6:17). He used His eyes to see (see 2 Nephi 9:44).

What is incredibly interesting, however, is the power of the sum total of His parts. It's much like 1 Kings 19:11–12 when Elijah looked to find Jehovah and was told,

> Go forth, and stand upon the mount before the Lord. And, behold, the Lord passed by, and a great and strong wind rent the mountains, and brake in pieces the rocks before the Lord; *but* the Lord *was* not in the wind: and after the wind an earthquake; *but* the Lord *was* not in the earthquake:
>
> And after the earthquake a fire; *but* the Lord *was* not in the fire: and after the fire a still small voice.

In the Book of Mormon, scribes tell of the Lord also speaking with a still, small voice (see 1 Nephi 17:45), a still voice of perfect mildness (see Helaman 5:30). In that tone of voice, real power is evident. When wickedness dominated the Nephite culture, the Lord spoke with a voice of a great tumultuous noise, "like unto the voice of thunder, which did cause the earth to shake as if it were to divide asunder" (see 1 Nephi 17:45). Although the tone of the voice varied greatly from the still, small voice, the power was the same.

Likewise, the Lord's eyes penetrate all. For example, with His all-searching eye, the Lord looked into a man's heart and knew who he really was (see 2 Nephi 9:44). Thus, when you consider the power and majesty of the total sum of the parts, the conclusion reached must include the fact that the Lord shows forth in myriad ways His infinite love for His children.

CHAPTER FIVE
JESUS CHRIST REVEALS HIMSELF AS THE ETERNAL JUDGE

I am brought forth triumphant through the air,
to meet you before the pleasing bar of the great Jehovah,
the Eternal Judge of both quick and dead.
(Moroni 10:34)

THE FINAL TITLE BY WHICH the Lord is known in the Book of Mormon is found in the last verse of Moroni: "And now I bid unto all, farewell. I soon go to rest in the paradise of God." In my personal study, I underlined the title *God* and assured myself that this was one of the most frequent titles for Christ in the Book of Mormon.

As the verse continues, Moroni expresses his confidence in being "brought forth triumphant through the air, to meet you before the pleasing bar of the great Jehovah." I had seen the title *Jehovah* before and routinely underlined this name for Christ, making a mental note that this title most often appears in the Old Testament. It was not until I read "the Eternal Judge of both quick and dead" that the 101st title by which Christ is known in the Book of Mormon was revealed (Moroni 10:34).

I had wanted the last verse to end with the title *Savior, Redeemer,* or *Deliverer,* a reminder of the Atonement of Jesus Christ and His mercy. It was startling to me that the Book of Mormon ended with the title *Eternal Judge.*

Having grown up with Perry Mason as a favorite television series, I knew that pleasing the judge was all-important and that a stern or merciful verdict had as much to do with the judge's nature as the client's innocence or guilt. I also knew that having an able advocate to speak of the client's innocence was all-important. As I pondered a courtroom scene and the nature of God as the Eternal Judge, I concluded that the answer to the puzzling issue of reward and punishment must be found in the Book of Mormon.

It was not a stretch for me to assume that when the Lord's children kept the commandments and ordinances, the Lord was pleased; when they rejected the commandments and ordinances, He was disappointed. What I had not realized was the gradations of the assumption.

Chapters in the Book of Mormon are filled with seemingly endless illustrations of the lovingkindness, longsuffering, and infinite goodness of the Lord toward His ancient people. For example, it was the Lord who guided Lehi, the brother of Jared, and the people of Mulek to the promised land. It was the Lord who called prophets to serve among the carnal majority who hesitated to accept their message of a Beloved Savior and the saving ordinance of baptism. When the majority rejected the word of God and the saving ordinances, God punished them with war, famine, pestilence, and poverty. Recognizing their hopeless state, the ancients repented and embraced the prophetic teachings of salvation. But as the elements calmed and the weapons of war retreated, carnality again dominated their civilization.

Wanting to determine if there was a causal effect—divine reward or punishment based on the acceptance or rejection of the word of God—I considered the question posed by the Prophet Joseph Smith in 1844: "I want to ask this congregation, every man, woman and child, to answer the question in their own hearts, what kind of a being God is?"[14] Without doubt, Joseph Smith knew the answer by divine revelation. He also knew that each Latter-day Saint in that congregation needed to have a true knowledge of the nature of God.

The best place to discover the nature of God is in the Book of Mormon. References to the Lord's nature are found in 320 verses. These verses speak of the merciful nature of God 221 times and of the judgmental nature of God 99 times. Although the numbers statistically reveal that the Lord showed forth on a two-to-one basis more attributes of a merciful, loving nature than a judgmental nature to the ancient peoples of America, it is the anecdotal accounts of the merciful nature of God that illuminate the character of Christ. Perry Mason would have liked the statistical odds. The statistics are significant, for they reveal that even though the ancient people and their civilizations failed on many levels, the Lord was more merciful than judgmental. Thus, it can be assumed that Jesus Christ as Eternal Judge will be more merciful than judgmental at the eternal bar of justice.

---

14 Ibid.

But now for the idea of gradation. When the ancient people kept the commandments, gave willing service to others, and set their course toward eternal life, the emotions God revealed varied from love (see 1 Nephi 11:22) to goodness (see 1 Nephi 1:1), and from comfort (see 2 Nephi 8:3) to patience (see Mosiah 4:6). The strictness with which the people turned their hearts, minds, and devotions to the Lord determined the extent, the degree, and the receipt of the Lord's loving attributes (see 4 Nephi).

When the ancient Book of Mormon people were not valiant and yet had not hardened their hearts, the Lord showed forth abundant offers of mercy, the blessing of time to repent, and the loving leadership of mighty prophets. The Lord even extended His arms of mercy into the night of darkened hearts and wandering minds.

Yet in each case, whether the ancient people lived in strict obedience to the laws and ordinances of God or were less than valiant, descriptions of the Lord's loving nature was not diluted or of one hue. There was always a full palette, a wide range of divine emotions to be discovered. When the Lord showed forth love, patience, or mercy, the emotion was always appropriate, controlled, and directed to bless the lives of His children.

The key to unlocking the abundance of God's love is strict obedience to the laws and ordinances of the gospel. The bottom line is, the man whose heart is broken and who has faith in Jesus Christ will feel the gradations of God's love.

The following shows the gradations of the loving descriptions of God.

Loving Descriptions of God

    Comfort—2 Nephi 8:3
        Comforted—1 Nephi 21:13
        Comfortedst—2 Nephi 22:1
        Comforteth—2 Nephi 8:12
        Compassion—Mosiah 15:9
        Pity—Ether 3:3

    Goodness—1 Nephi 1:1
        Exceeding Goodness—Alma 60:11
        Good—Moroni 7:12
        Great Goodness—2 Nephi 4:17

Great Infinite Goodness—Helaman 12:1
Immediate Goodness—Mosiah 25:10
Infinite Goodness—2 Nephi 1:10

Joy—2 Nephi 19:17
Pleased—Mosiah 14:10
Pleasure—Jacob 4:9
Rejoice Exceedingly—Jacob 5:60

Love—1 Nephi 11:22
Loved—Helaman 15:3
Loveth—1 Nephi 11:17
Loving Kindness—1 Nephi 19:9
Matchless Bounty of His Love—Alma 26:15

Mercy—1 Nephi 1:14
Abundant Mercy—Alma 18:41
Exceedingly Merciful—Jarom 1:3
Great Mercy—Jacob 4:10
Greatness of the Mercy—2 Nephi 9:19
Infinite Mercy—Mosiah 28:4
Mercies—2 Nephi 1:2
Merciful—1 Nephi 1:14
Multitude of His Tender Mercies—1 Nephi 8:8
Pure Mercies—Moroni 8:19
Tender Mercies—1 Nephi 1:20

Patience—Mosiah 4:6
Long-suffering—Mosiah 4:11

Not all descendants of Lehi experienced the loving descriptions of God, for they had hardened their hearts against the sacred. They "lift[ed] up their heads in wickedness . . . to commit whoredoms" (Alma 30:18), pressing the adulterous to lasciviousness and uncontrolled passions (see Alma 45:11–13) and pressing the angry to avenging hatred (see Mormon 3:9–11). They "despise[ed] others, turned their backs upon the needy and the naked and those who were hungry, and those who were athirst, and those who were sick and afflicted" (Alma 4:12). They heaped "oppression [upon] the poor . . . smiting their humble brethren upon the cheek, making a mock of that which was sacred, denying the spirit of prophecy and of revelation" (Helaman 4:12). And they sought "for power, and authority, and riches, and the vain things of the world" (3 Nephi 6:15).

Their hearts did not rejoice in the abundance of God's blessings, for they were set in an idolatrous way "upon gold, and upon silver, and upon all manner of fine goods" (Alma 31:24). It could be said that they sold "themselves for naught" (2 Nephi 26:10). A direct consequence of their willful choice of wrongdoing was the loss of earthly joys and eternal blessings.

When the ancient people of the Book of Mormon flagrantly rebelled against the counsel of God and lived in wickedness and attempted to thwart the gospel plan, the Lord was displeased (see 2 Nephi 1:22), angry (see 1 Nephi 20:9), and full of wrath (see 1 Nephi 13:11). The degree to which the people disobeyed the laws and ordinances of God determined their judgment (see Alma 36:15). When the majority rejected God and willfully rebelled against His prophets, they faced the fiery indignation, fierce anger, and almighty wrath of the Lord. The following shows the gradations of the judgmental descriptions of God.

Judgmental Descriptions of God

Anger—1 Nephi 20:9
    Angry—1 Nephi 18:10
    Fierce Anger—2 Nephi 23:9
    Fiery Indignation—Alma 40:14
    Fury—2 Nephi 8:20

Chasten—1 Nephi 16:39
    Chastened—1 Nephi 16:39
    Rebuke—2 Nephi 8:20

Displeasure—2 Nephi 1:22
    Anguish—Mosiah 3:7
    Grief—Mosiah 14:10
    Grieveth—Jacob 5:51
    Jealous—Mosiah 11:22
    Sorrows—Mosiah 14:3
    Suffer—Mosiah 8:20
    Suffereth—Alma 7:13
    Sufferings—Mosiah 18:2

Troubled—3 Nephi 17:14
　　　Vengeance—Mormon 3:15
　　　Wept—Jacob 5:41

Wrath—1 Nephi 13:11
　　　Almighty Wrath—Alma 54:6
　　　Cup of the Wrath—Mosiah 3:26
　　　Fulness of His Wrath—1 Nephi 22:17
　　　Fulness of My Wrath—Ether 9:20
　　　Fulness of the Wrath—1 Nephi 22:16

There is a dramatic difference between chastening, anguish, fiery indignation, and the fulness of God's wrath. But there is not a gradation when it comes to the reasons for being blessed or punished. The consistent pattern in the Book of Mormon is this: Obedience to the laws and ordinances of the gospel brings blessings of God. Disobedience and willful rebellion bring God's judgmental wrath. The choice for man is clear—live to receive a divine reward or live to receive divine punishment.

But regardless of man's choice, the choice is always a matter of the heart. The descendants of Lehi whose hearts were broken, "groane[d]" (2 Nephi 4:19), were "weighed down with sorrow" (2 Nephi 1:17), and wept (see 2 Nephi 4:26), being "pained" (1 Nephi 17:47). They experienced lowliness (see Moroni 7:44) as their hearts melted (see 2 Nephi 23:7) and became softened (see 1 Nephi 2:16). In so doing, they had a "mighty change" of heart (Alma 5:12). With fresh courage (see Alma 15:4), renewed energy (see Moroni 7:48), and a desire for oneness with God (see 2 Nephi 1:21), Lehi's descendants turned to the Lord in righteousness (see 2 Nephi 9:49) and became magnified (see 2 Nephi 25:13), purified (see Jacob 2:10), and "full of thanks" (Alma 37:37).

Knowing something of the divine nature of God and the final name by which Jesus is known in the Book of Mormon makes it easier to determine the desired outcome of life, for the judgments of God have been consistent whether they were toward Father Lehi on his voyage to the promised land or the Jaredites in barges. Those who kept the commandments of God were blessed, and those who did not had no such blessings.

Never once was the Eternal Judge swayed by excuses, rationale, or logic games. The conniving Korihor or Nehor did not stand a chance against God's laws and holy prophets. The only hope for redemption to such strict laws and ordinances is Jesus Christ, our Advocate with the Father. Because of the Atonement of Jesus Christ, inheriting eternal life is within the reach of all.

CHAPTER SIX
CENTRAL MESSAGE OF CHRIST

*I have drunk out of that bitter cup which the Father hath given me,
and have glorified the Father in taking upon me the sins of the world,
in the which I have suffered the will of the Father
in all things from the beginning.*
(3 Nephi 11:11)

Knowing something of the frequency with which the name of Jesus Christ appears in the Book of Mormon and the various titles by which He is known suggests that Christ is not only the main character in the Book of Mormon but has a central message for the readers. He is not like Lehi in his generation, Captain Moroni in his, or the sons of Helaman in theirs—people who enter the text and exit before the manuscript ends. Christ appears in the first verse in the Book of Mormon (see 1 Nephi 1:1) and in every chapter and nearly every verse throughout the text, including the last verse (see Moroni 10:34).

Being curious by nature, I searched to find the central message presented of Christ that all other messages of Him could appendage to. In other words, in a period of about a thousand years (600 BC to AD 421) in which generations come and go, lifestyles change, governments convulse, and wars tear families apart, was there one message that was consistently repeated? I presumed that if there was a main message, it would have to do with the hope-filled promise that Jesus Christ would visit His people in the Western hemisphere or that it would be the most important teaching from His mortal ministry in biblical lands.

Although I found promises that Christ would manifest himself in the Americas from the book of First Nephi to the words of Samuel the Lamanite, there were not enough instances to prove that His manifestation was the central theme. I then searched to find whether my second guess—a teaching from his mortal ministry near the shores of Galilee and in Jerusalem—was more viable.

The natural place for me to start was with Mary, the mother of Jesus. I found that Nephi saw in vision the prophesied virgin "in the city of Nazareth" (1 Nephi 11:13). An angel asked Nephi, "What beholdest thou?" (1 Nephi 11:14). "A virgin, most beautiful and fair above all other virgins," he replied (1 Nephi 11:15). The angel testified to Nephi, "Behold, the virgin whom thou seest is the mother of the Son of God" (1 Nephi 11:18). King Benjamin announced her name—"And his mother shall be called Mary" (Mosiah 3:8). In that announcement, Mary became the first and only woman in holy writ mentioned by name before her birth. Years later, Alma echoed King Benjamin's words: "And behold, he shall be born of Mary" (Alma 7:10). As it turned out, however, although prophetic scribes wrote of Mary in the Book of Mormon, she was not their central message.

I then turned to the birth of Jesus, the most celebrated event in all Christendom. In a cave on the hillside of Bethlehem, "the days were accomplished that [Mary] should be delivered. And she brought forth her firstborn son" (Luke 2:6–7). Like generations of Jewish mothers before her, Mary wrapped her newborn in swaddling clothes. Unlike most Jewish mothers, however, she had no crib for her babe. Improvising, Mary "laid him in a manger" (Luke 2:7). As the story goes, on that night of nights the glory of the Lord shone round about the shepherds, and "they were sore afraid" (Luke 2:9). "Fear not: for, behold, I bring you good tidings of great joy, which shall be to all people," announced an angel. "For unto you is born this day in the city of David, a Saviour, which is Christ the Lord" (Luke 2:10–11). Although this is a favorite story from the life of Jesus, it proved not to be the dominant message of Christ in the Book of Mormon.

I then searched references to John the Baptist. I thought surely the message of John—*repent*—shouted in a society where class distinction, fine-twined linen, and a self-serving embrace of the sacred were all too apparent was the main message. I figured his message was still timely. John's urgent plea was to turn from the blatant ills of the Palestinian society. His pressing invitation was to embrace the sacred—the covenants between Jehovah and the fathers of Israel. But once again, neither John the Baptist nor his message proved to be the theme of Christ in the Book of Mormon.

The same could be said for the baptism of Jesus, temptations in the wilderness, choosing the Twelve Apostles, doctrinal teachings in

Galilee, and His death and Resurrection. But with this said, I need to make clear that centuries before the resurrected Lord appeared in the Americas, Book of Mormon prophetic scribes did write of His baptism (see 2 Nephi 31:4), His ministry (see 2 Nephi 2:4), His disciples (see 1 Nephi 1:10), His suffering and death (see 1 Nephi 10:11), and His Resurrection (see 2 Nephi 2:8).

Below is a brief summation of how frequently the Book of Mormon prophetic scribes wrote of events that occurred in Christ's earthly ministry prior to His birth in Bethlehem. What will catch your eye is the central message—the Atonement of Jesus Christ.

Central Message in the Book of Mormon Prior to Christ's Birth

Number of References:

Manifestation in the Western Hemisphere—39
Son of the Eternal Father—2
Mary the Mother of Jesus—10
Birth—12
John the Baptist—6
Baptism—9
Choosing Twelve—6
Ministry—15
Atonement—101
Suffering and Death—44
Resurrection—34

Is it really surprising that of all the miracles of Christ and of all His doctrinal teachings, the central message is the Atonement? Of that Atonement, the Prophet Joseph Smith said, "All other things, are only appendages to these, which pertain to our religion."[15] The same can be said of the Book of Mormon—all the teachings of Jesus Christ in the Book of Mormon are appendages to the Atonement.

With this understanding, let us learn together why the Atonement is the central message. The answer is, the Atonement has always been the central message. The Atonement of Jesus Christ was first introduced in the Garden of Eden when the Lord God spoke to the serpent, the "prime

---

[15] "History, 1838–1856, volume B-1 [1 September 1834–2 November 1838]," 796, *The Joseph Smith Papers*, Church History Library, Salt Lake City.

mover in the transgression" of Adam and Eve.[16] With a voice of certain clarity and divine judgment, "The Lord God said unto the serpent, Because thou hast done this, thou *art* cursed above all cattle, and above every beast of the field; upon thy belly shalt thou go, and dust shalt thou eat all the days of thy life" (Genesis 3:14; see also Moses 4:20). Whatever the serpent's stature had been before enticing Eve to partake of the forbidden fruit—whether tall or short, straight or bent—the serpent became the "basest of animals," physically repulsive.[17] God's judgment—"upon thy belly shalt thou go, and dust shalt thou eat all the days of thy life" (Genesis 3:14)—changed the physical stature of the serpent forever. No longer would the serpent appear as the most "subtle" of God's creatures. To be condemned to eat or "lick the dust" was a mark of degradation upon the serpent then and for centuries to come (see Psalms 72:9; Isaiah 49:23).[18] No one, not even a serpent, can appear high and mighty when licking the dust for food.

The judgment upon the serpent was not complete nor would it ever be without an announcement of the plan of salvation with the Atonement of Jesus Christ at its core. The Lord said to the serpent, "I will put enmity between thee and the woman, and between thy seed and her seed; it shall bruise thy head, and thou shalt bruise his heel" (Genesis 3:15; see also Moses 4:21). *Enmity*, with all the friction and hostility that accompanies such associations, would now epitomize the relationship between the serpent and Eve as well as all unborn generations. If you look for evidence of such enmity, you'll see on nearly every page of the Old and New Testaments that man fights against man, and women and children suffer. There was to be no peace and harmony between Satan and the woman or her offspring as long as time held sway. But then the Lord God pronounced the final blow upon the serpent: "It shall bruise thy head, and thou shalt bruise his heel" (Genesis 3:15). What appears at first glance the bruising of another's body was in actuality an announcement of the triumphal victory of Jesus Christ over the serpent.

Although it may appear odd that the victory of Christ over Satan would first appear in the Lord's judgment upon the serpent, it is not odd. The placement of Christ in the judgment scene has much more to do with the redemption of God's authority than a direct promise to

---

[16] Reverend J. R. Dummelow, *A Commentary on the Holy Bible* (New York: MacMillan, 1908), 10.

[17] Nehama Aschkenasy, *Eve's Journey: Feminine Images in Hebraic Literary Tradition* (Philadelphia: University of Pennsylvania Press, 1986), 45.

[18] Dummelow, *Commentary on the Holy Bible*, 10.

Adam and Eve—or, as Ezekiel 36:22 states, "Thus saith the Lord God; I do not this for your sakes . . . but for mine holy name's sake"[19]

If there is still confusion, the Apostle Paul adds clarity in his writings to the Romans: "And the God of peace shall bruise Satan under your feet" (Romans 16:20; see also Genesis 3:15; Moses 4:21). The implication of these scriptural passages is as follows: While man and woman will suffer satanic bruises, their Savior Jesus Christ, as the "seed of the woman," will bruise the serpent's head, meaning the very foundation of Hell.[20] In that pronouncement—that glorious pronouncement—the Lord God introduced Adam and Eve to the plan of salvation—a plan centered on the Atonement of Jesus Christ (see Alma 42:8; Alma 34:9).[21]

As the centuries passed, a celebration was held each year to remember the promise of the Atonement. It was called the Day of Atonement, the holiest day of the year to the Jewish people. On that day, a temple priest led a goat—a scapegoat—with a red sash tied to its horns and a placard that read *La-Azazel* around its neck through the Porch of Solomon out the eastern gate to the Mount of Olives, and from there into the wilderness where the goat was set free. This action symbolized that through the Atonement, sins would vanish and man was free of sin, and as such he could return to his Maker.[22] The Israelites celebrated on the Day of Atonement what Isaiah had prophesied many years before: "Surely he has borne our griefs and carried our sorrows. . . . All we like sheep have gone astray, we have turned every one to his own way; and the Lord hath laid on him the iniquity of us all" (Isaiah 53:4, 6).

Although the house of Israel longed for a Redeemer to take their sins, few knew that it was Jesus of Nazareth who fulfilled their longings. It happened on the night of Seder—*Leil Shimurim*, meaning "night of the watchers"—in Passover Week. It was the night when Jewish men were admonished to stay awake and watch for God to save His people.

On that night Jesus and His disciples were in the Upper Room. His disciples heard Jesus pray, "Father, the hour is come; glorify thy Son,

---

[19] Reverend Derek Kidner, *Tyndale Old Testament Commentary—Genesis: An Introduction and Commentary* (London: IVP Academic Press, 1967), 70–71.
[20] Dummelow, *Commentary on the Holy Bible*, 10.
[21] See Jay E. Jensen, "Keep an Eternal Perspective," *Ensign*, May 2000.
[22] See Alfred Edersheim, *The Temple: Its Ministry and Services as They Were at the Time of Jesus Christ* (Grand Rapids: Wm. B. Eerdmans Publishing, 1994), 318–319; James E. Talmage, *Jesus the Christ* (Salt Lake City: Deseret Book, 1983), 465; Bruce R. McConkie, *Doctrinal New Testament Commentary: The Gospels*, vol. 1 (Salt Lake City: Bookcraft, 1988), 489.

that thy Son also may glorify thee" (John 17:1). In that prayer, Jesus offered Himself as a ransom for the sins of the world, announced the completion of His mortal ministry, and pled with His Father in behalf of His faithful Apostles and those who will believe in their teachings (see John 17).[23]

Jesus and His disciples then left the Upper Room and walked to the Mount of Olives, a mile-long chain of hills about three hundred feet from Jerusalem (see Acts 1:12). Of the three prominent summits on the hills—the Mount of Scopus, the Mount of Scandal, and the Mount of Offense—it was on Mount Scopus, which in Greek means "lookout point" and in Hebrew means "mount of the watchman," that Jesus paused in the Garden of Gethsemane, a garden where olive trees had thrived for centuries with little care even during long periods of drought.

Jesus turned to His disciples Peter, James, and John and asked them to follow Him into a secluded area of Gethsemane and there watch while He went "about a stone's cast" or about a hundred feet away, and knelt in supplication to His Father (Luke 22:41). Jesus knew this was His appointed hour—the hour for which He had come into the world (see John 12:27). This hour He would take upon Himself the sins of the world. For this purpose was He born, and for this purpose had He lived.[24]

How long Jesus was away from Peter, James, and John is not known. The Jews divided the night into three periods—sunset to midnight, midnight to cockcrow, and cockcrow to sunrise. The Greco-Roman world divided the night into four military watches of about three hours each (see Mark 6:48; Luke 12:38). The first watch began at sundown, about six in the evening. The second watch began when the moon was halfway up in the sky. The third watch began when the moon reached the zenith, and the fourth watch began when the moon was halfway down in the sky, about six in the morning. Because of the two systems for counting time, it is difficult to calculate the hours Jesus was away from Peter, James, and John in Gethsemane.[25]

Yet it is known that during those hours Jesus atoned for the sins, sorrows, and sickness of the world. We cannot begin to comprehend the magnitude of those hours, for—

---

[23] See Bruce R. McConkie, *The Mortal Messiah: From Bethlehem to Calvary*, 4 vols. (Salt Lake City: Deseret Book, 1981), 109, 111; see also McConkie, *Doctrinal Commentary*, 760.

[24] See Alexander B. Morrison, "For This Cause Came I into the World," *Ensign*, November 1999.

[25] William Smith, *The New Smith's Bible Dictionary*, Reuel G. Lemmons, ed. (Garden City, New York: Doubleday & Company, 1966), 260.

> there is no mystery to compare with the mystery of redemption, not even the mystery of creation. Finite minds can no more comprehend how and in what manner Jesus performed his redeeming labors than they can comprehend how matter came into being, or how Gods began to be. . . . We may not intrude too closely into this scene. It is shrouded in a halo and a mystery into which no footstep may penetrate.[26]

Yet we know that in Gethsemane, Jesus descended below all things as he prepared himself to rise above them all. Jesus "suffered the pain of all men, that all men might repent and come unto him."[27] We also know that His prayer, "O my Father, if it be possible, let this cup pass from me" was a metaphor meaning "that which is allotted by God, whether blessing or judgment" (Matthew 26:39; see Psalms 16:5; Psalms 116:13).[28]

In the Garden of Gethsemane, Jesus accepted the judgment of God and became the Savior, the Redeemer of the World. Because of that singular, infinite Atonement, we are ransomed from the effects of the Fall of Adam, and spiritual and temporal death are overcome through Christ, our victorious Deliverer.

The details of the Atonement presented in the New Testament are sparse and limited to only a few verses, whereas stories of healing lepers and raising Lazarus from the dead are more descriptive. If readers of the New Testament are not careful, the magnitude of the Atonement of Jesus Christ in the Garden of Gethsemane could be overlooked.

This is not so for readers of the Book of Mormon. The Book of Mormon is replete with verses about the Atonement. For example, in the book of Second Nephi, we learn that the Savior offered Himself as a sacrifice for sin to answer the ends of the law and that the Atonement is infinite and satisfies the demands of justice. We learn in the book of Jacob that the only way for you and me to be reconciled unto God is through the Atonement, and if there had been no Atonement, all mankind would be lost. In the book of Mosiah, we learn that the law of Moses avails nothing except through the Atonement. In the book

---

[26] McConkie, *The Mortal Messiah*, 4:124, 127.
[27] McConkie, *The Mortal Messiah*, 4:128; D&C 18:11.
[28] Smith, *Bible Dictionary*, 76; Raymond E. Brown, *The Death of the Messiah: From Gethsemane to the Grave—A Commentary on the Passion Narratives in the Four Gospels* (New York: Doubleday, 1994), 163–178.

of Alma, we learn that the Atonement was not only for sin, but that Jesus took upon Himself the pains and sickness of His people. We also learn that the Atonement brings to pass the resurrection. The book of Helaman unlocks the mystery of the Atonement, assuring us that the only means whereby man can be saved is through the atoning blood of Jesus Christ. And the book of Moroni assures us that we are sanctified in Christ by the grace of His Atonement. Thus, by reading the Book of Mormon, you and I learn in plainness and depth the sacred purpose of the Atonement of Jesus Christ.

I have learned from the ancient prophetic scribes that when I don't have the inner strength to forgive, the Atonement of Jesus Christ fills in what I lack. Rather than share a personal story, this is best illustrated in a story told by Elder Gerrit W. Gong at general conference in May 2016:

> A young woman in another country applied to work as a journalist, but the official who assigned jobs was merciless. He said to her, "With my signature, I guarantee you will not become a journalist but will dig sewers." She was the only woman digging sewers in a gang of men.
>
> Years later this woman became an official. One day a man came in needing her signature for a job.
>
> She asked, "Do you remember me?" He did not.
>
> She said, "You do not remember me, but I remember you. With your signature, you guaranteed I never became a journalist. With your signature, you sent me to dig sewers, the only woman in a gang of men."
>
> She told me, "I feel I should treat that man better than he treated me—but I do not have that strength."

Elder Gong concluded, "Sometimes that strength is not within us, but it can be found in remembering the Atonement of our Savior, Jesus Christ."[29]

The Book of Mormon teaches me that when I stumble and fail to keep the commandments of God, the Atonement of Jesus Christ covers my wrongs. President Gordon B. Hinckley taught this principle by relating a type of parable that occurred in a one-room schoolhouse in the back mountains of Virginia:

---

[29] Gerrit W. Gong, "Always Remember Him," *Ensign*, May 2016.

The first day of school the teacher asked the boys to establish their own rules and the penalty for breaking the rules. The class came up with 10 rules, which were written on the blackboard. Then the teacher asked, "What shall we do with one who breaks the rules?"

"Beat him across the back ten times without his coat on," came the response.

A day or so later, . . . the lunch of a big student, named Tom, was stolen. The thief was located—a little hungry fellow, about ten years old.

As Little Jim came up to take his licking, he pleaded to keep his coat on.

"Take your coat off," the teacher said. "You helped make the rules!"

The boy took off the coat. He had no shirt and revealed a bony little crippled body. As the teacher hesitated with the rod, Big Tom jumped to his feet and volunteered to take the boy's licking.

"Very well, there is a certain law that one can become a substitute for another. Are you all agreed?" the teacher asked.

After five strokes across Tom's back, the rod broke. The class was sobbing. Little Jim had reached up and caught Tom with both arms around his neck. "Tom, I'm sorry that I stole your lunch, but I was awful hungry. Tom, I will love you till I die for taking my licking for me! Yes, I will love you forever!"

President Hinckley then quoted Isaiah: "Surely he hath borne our griefs, and carried our sorrows.... He was wounded for our transgressions, he was bruised for our iniquities: the chastisement of our peace was upon him; and with his stripes we are healed" (Isaiah 53:4–5).[30]

I profess that the central message of the Book of Mormon is the Atonement of Jesus Christ. It was Jesus who ransomed "men from the

---

[30] Gordon B. Hinckley, "The Wondrous and True Story of Christmas," *Ensign*, December 2000, quoted in James E. Faust, "The Atonement: Our Greatest Hope," *Ensign*, November 2001.

temporal and spiritual death brought upon them by the fall of Adam."[31] He "cam to satisfy the demands of divine justice and to bring mercy to the penitent.[32] What I have learned from the repetitive message in the Book of Mormon is that Jesus is my Savior, Deliverer, Mediator, and Intercessor not only when I die, but as I live each day. Through the infinite Atonement of Jesus, there is hope for the downtrodden, joy for the oppressed, peace for the weary, and salvation for the children of God.

---

[31] Bruce R. McConkie, "Come, Know the Lord Jesus," *Ensign*, May 1997.
[32] Ibid.

CHAPTER SEVEN
A PERSONAL WITNESS OF CHRIST

God said unto Moses, I AM THAT I AM.
(Exodus 3:14)

A LITTLE GIRL WAS DRAWING a picture with crayons when her teacher walked by and asked her what she was doing. The little girl stated with self-assurance that she was drawing a picture of God. The teacher was amused and taken back. She told the little girl that no one knows what God looks like, to which the little girl calmly replied: "They will when I am finished."[33]

This story illustrates how few, not even the little girl's teacher, believe it is possible to see Deity.

How grateful I am that the Book of Mormon scribes wrote not only of holy men living in the Western hemisphere that have known of, spoken of, and written of Christ, but of those holy prophets who personally saw my Redeemer. The brother of Jared saw in vision the Lord and heard, "Behold, I am Jesus Christ" (Ether 3:14). In a revelatory dream, Father Lehi "saw One descending out of the midst of heaven" (1 Nephi 1:9). And in his youth, Jacob was privileged to behold the glory of God (see 2 Nephi 2:4).

Nineteen other men referred to by name in the Book of Mormon also saw the Christ: King Emer (see Ether 9:22), Ether (see Ether 13:4), Nephi (see 1 Nephi 11:1), King Lamoni (see Alma 19:13), Alma (see Alma 36:22), Mormon (see Mormon 1:15), Moroni (see Ether 12:39), Nephi (brother to Timothy), Timothy, Jonas, Mathoni, Mathonihah, Kumen, Kumenonhi, Jeremiah, Shemnon, Jonas, Zedekiah, and Isaiah

---

[33] Binford Winston Gilbert, *The Pastoral Care of Depression: A Guidebook* (New York: Haworth Pastoral Press, 1998), 76.

(see 3 Nephi 19:4). In total, three of these men were Jaredites, and eighteen were descendants of Father Lehi, who also saw his Redeemer.

Looking at these men as a whole, I can discover four instructive parallels between Christ's separate appearances to the three Jaredites and to the eighteen descendants of Father Lehi. First, the founders of each civilization—the brother of Jared (see Ether 3:6–15) and Lehi (see 1 Nephi 1:8–9)—saw Christ before arriving in the promised land. Second, a king in each culture saw the Christ: Emer (see Ether 9:22) and Lamoni (see Alma 19:13). Third, the last known prophet of each civilization received a manifestation of Jesus Christ: Ether (see Ether 13:4) and Moroni (see Ether 12:39). And fourth, within both cultures, unnumbered people saw the Lord: the Jaredites (see Ether 12:19) and the multitude near the temple in the land of Bountiful (see 3 Nephi 11:16–17).

Those who saw Christ were unique in their generation. The same could be said in our generation. Beginning with the First Vision of Joseph Smith in the Sacred Grove in Palmyra, holy men have been privileged to see our Savior and converse with Him.

If you were to line up all scripture and all the holy men and women who have ever seen Christ, there is only one scriptural account of a large multitude of men, women, and children seeing the resurrected Lord. The account recorded in the Book of Mormon stands alone in holy writ, for never before or since has a multitude received such a sure witness of the identity of Jesus Christ.

You may ask, "What of the Savior's mortality and ministry in the land of Jerusalem? After all, didn't multitudes press against Him and have the privilege of seeing Him?" To answer the question, let us reason together. In the land of Jerusalem, there is no question that the Beloved Son of God was born (see Matthew 1:23), baptized (see Matthew 3:13), crucified (see Matthew 20:19), and resurrected (see Mark 16:9). Yet most of the multitudes who saw and heard Him in biblical lands did not know His true identity. They were "astonished [during his youth] at his understanding and answers" (Luke 2:47), acknowledged him as a healer (see Mark 1:40–45), feasted on the food He procured (see John 6:5–14), and marveled at His casting out of devils from the besieged (see Mark 9:25). Yet to them, Jesus was not the Son of God; He was a healer, a teacher, a miracle worker (see Luke 4:24).

Their sight was clouded and their hearing impaired, for they did not open their spiritual eyes to ascertain His true identity. An exception to this general lack of understanding was the Apostle Peter: "[Jesus] saith unto them, But whom say ye that I am? And Simon Peter answered and said, Thou art the Christ, the Son of the living God" (Matthew 16:15–16).

Like Peter, the Book of Mormon multitude clearly saw, heard, and acknowledged Jesus Christ as the Son of God, their Redeemer. The multitude also witnessed the ushering in of a new dispensation founded on the doctrine of Christ and were "all converted unto the Lord, upon all the face of the land" (4 Nephi 1:2). For nearly two hundred years, they enjoyed continuous peace and prosperity (see 4 Nephi 1:22–23).

The unique story of twenty-five hundred people "consist[ing] of men, women, and children" witnessing Christ in the Americas is the centerpiece of the Book of Mormon (3 Nephi 17:25). The year of their witness was AD 34, a year that requires thirty-seven pages in the Book of Mormon to complete, and the place was near the temple in the land of Bountiful. It appears this multitude had gathered as families with their "sick and their afflicted, and their lame, and with their blind, and with their dumb, and with all them that were afflicted in any manner" (3 Nephi 17:9).

The witness begins as the multitude were conversing one with another on two topics that dominated their conversation. The first concerned the changes that had taken place on the earth (see 3 Nephi 11:1): the great city of Zarahemla had been burned with fire (see 3 Nephi 8:8), the city of Moroni had sunk in the depths of the sea (see 3 Nephi 8:9), the city of Moronihah had been covered with earth (see 3 Nephi 8:10), and highways had been broken up (see 3 Nephi 8:13). It was, in essence, a conversation about "the face of the whole earth [becoming] deformed" (3 Nephi 8:17). The second topic of conversation was of more eternal importance: the "sign [which] had been given concerning [Christ's] death" (3 Nephi 11:2).

Notably, no one person appears to have conducted the flow of conversation. There was not a speaker or a tower to look at, as with King Benjamin (see Mosiah 2). No one appeared to be presiding, conducting, or speaking, even though the prophet Nephi was among their number (see 3 Nephi 11:18). It was as if they were conversing, waiting, as it were, for a meeting to begin or waiting to know for what purpose they had come to the temple with their families at that particular time.

Any question of who was to preside was put to rest when God the Father addressed the gathering (see 3 Nephi 11:3). He did not wait for silence or for their attention as they conversed one with another. The multitude heard a piercing voice out of heaven but could not understand the audible message. A second time they heard the voice, but again they did not understand it (see 3 Nephi 11:4). Was it because the Lord did not speak plainly? No, it was because the people needed the veil over their minds and hearts removed.

The divine parental voice spoke a third time, and this time the assembly understood: "Behold my Beloved Son, in whom I am well pleased, in whom I have glorified my name—hear ye him" (3 Nephi 11:7). The multitude gazed toward heaven to hear the words of God the Father, and in their gazing became witnesses of the glorious descent of Jesus Christ to the land of Bountiful (see 3 Nephi 11:8).

Although the veil had been lifted from the people's minds, ears, and eyes—for they could understand the voice and see the personage—their understanding was yet clouded. The multitude wrongfully concluded that the man clothed in white and descending toward them was an angel, not Jesus Christ of whom the prophets had testified (see 3 Nephi 11:8). I pause to ask myself, *Had they not read the words of holy prophets?* Why did this mistaken identity occur? Perhaps the multitude had known *of Him* but did not *know Him*.

An exception was the prophet Nephi, who had previously received the gift to know (see 3 Nephi 7:15). Was it Nephi, then, who increased their enlightenment? No, it was their Savior, their Redeemer, their God—Jesus the Christ. He announced, "Behold, I am Jesus Christ, whom the prophets testified shall come into the world" (3 Nephi 11:10).

The result of this announcement was not a shout for joy but what I term "sacred silence." As if the people needed further divine affirmation to understand the full import of the name, the risen Lord spoke of His earthly ministry in Jerusalem. He did not give information about His birth, His baptism, His choosing of the Twelve Apostles, His Crucifixion, or His Resurrection. Instead, He spoke of the Atonement, the central theme of the Book of Mormon: "[I] have glorified the Father in taking upon me the sins of this world, in the which I have suffered the will of the Father in all things from the beginning" (3 Nephi 11:11).

Why did the resurrected Lord speak of the Atonement to assure the multitude of His identity? It was because the Atonement was the central message of Christ's earthly ministry. It was because He wanted the multitude to know of His great gift to all. The Atonement is the thread that binds the plan of salvation. It is the most important doctrine of the gospel. Prophets, scribes, and writers of the Book of Mormon wrote of this doctrine more frequently than they wrote of any other single concept in the life of Jesus.

From this point on, the multitude knew who was presiding and who was conducting. They were now prepared to learn why they had gathered near the temple at Bountiful. The purpose was not only to see Jesus as those in Jerusalem had seen Him, but to receive a sure witness that the man conducting this meeting was the very Christ, the Son of God, the Savior of the World.

In charitable magnitude, the resurrected Lord invited the multitude to come forward and become sure witnesses of Him. They were invited to thrust their hands into His side and feel the prints of the nails in His hands and feet (see 3 Nephi 11:14). Notice the verbs used—*thrust* and *feel*. The Savior added the sense of touch to the senses of sight and hearing already involved in the witnessing process. An experience involving only one sense, such as sight, might be counterfeited or in some other way remain open to question. But the three senses together were decisive—they led to a spiritual knowledge that went beyond the physical. They led to a sure witness of Jesus Christ.

The significance of touching the resurrected Lord is heightened as we contemplate the time Jesus spent with the multitude in offering this sacred privilege. If only twenty-five hundred people went "forth one by one until they had all gone forth, and did see with their eyes and did feel with their hands, and did know of a surety and did bear record" (3 Nephi 11:15), each taking five seconds, twelve people would complete the process in one minute. In one hour, at this rate, 720 people would be sure witnesses; in three hours, 2,260 people would have completed the process. What if each one took longer than five seconds? What if each person took ten seconds or a minute? Marvelous is the magnitude of the event at which the Savior presided, enabling a diverse multitude of families to share together the sacred privilege of touching their Redeemer.

Whatever the time involved, when it was completed, the multitude shouted in one accord, "Hosanna! Blessed be the name of the Most High God!" (3 Nephi 11:17). It is significant that the word *hosanna* is defined as "save now."[34] After the shout, the multitude fell "down at the feet of Jesus, and did worship him" (3 Nephi 11:17). A multitude now possessed a sure witness to what the prophets had testified since the beginning of time.

Although Christ now had a multitude of sure witnesses, there was only one man He called to come forward: "And it came to pass that he spake unto Nephi (for Nephi was among the multitude) and he

---

[34] "Hosanna," Bible Dictionary, 704–705.

commanded him that he should come forth. And Nephi arose and went forth, and bowed himself before the Lord and did kiss his feet" (3 Nephi 11:18–19).

Why was Nephi called to "come forth"? Before AD 34, Nephi had "been visited by angels and also the voice of the Lord, therefore having seen angels, and being eye-witness, and having had power given unto him that he might know concerning the ministry of Christ" (3 Nephi 7:15). Furthermore, he had gone forth and testified, "boldly, repentance and remission of sins through faith on the Lord Jesus Christ" (3 Nephi 7:16).

Nephi had ministered "with power and with great authority" (3 Nephi 7:17), even to the casting out of "devils and unclean spirits; and even his brother did he raise from the dead, after he had been stoned and suffered death by the people" (3 Nephi 7:19). Although there were now twenty-five hundred witnesses, it was still Nephi who was the Lord's prophet, and it was Nephi who was called forth.

As I have pondered the events of AD 34 as recorded in the Book of Mormon, I have wondered if they are but a prelude to the symphony that will play at the glorious Second Coming of Jesus Christ. Once again, in another era and at another place, multitudes consisting of men, women, and children will have the privilege of being witnesses that the resurrected Lord is their Deliverer and Messiah.

Ultimately, every knee shall bow and every tongue confess that Jesus is the Christ. Who will the Lord call to "come forth" from among the multitude? The prophet, of course. Instead of two hundred years passing away in peace and prosperity, as was the case following the ascension of the resurrected Lord, a thousand years will pass away in peace, joy, and love all over the world.

There is no question that Jesus Christ will come again. The question is, when He comes again will we be ready?

> I wonder, when he comes again,
> Will I be ready there
> To look upon his loving face
> And join with him in prayer?
> Each day I'll try to do his will
> And let my light so shine
> That others seeing me may seek
> For greater light divine.
> Then, when that blessed day is here,

He'll love me and he'll say,
"You've served me well, my little child;
Come unto my arms to stay."[35]

---

[35] "When He Comes Again," *Children's Songbook* (Salt Lake City: The Church of Jesus Christ of Latter-day Saints, 2002), 82; words and music by Mirla Greenwood Thayne, 1907–1997.

CHAPTER EIGHT
HIS THREE-DAY MINISTRY

*And he did expound all things, even from the beginning
until the time that he should come in his glory.*
(3 Nephi 26:3)

The Savior's ministry to the Nephites was more than the appearance of the resurrected Lord to the assembled in Bountiful that day. Although, at first glance it would seem that little could surpass the privilege of witnessing the Lord's descent from heaven—hearing His assuring words of Atonement or His command to "arise and come forth unto me, that ye may thrust your hands into my side, and also that ye may feel the prints of the nails in my hands and in my feet, that ye may know that I am the God of Israel" (3 Nephi 11:14)—it should be remembered that the Lord spent three consecutive days with the multitude, days filled with instruction, blessings, and ordinances. During those three days, what had been a mystery was made plain. What had been a physical ailment was healed. The multitude, who had a sure knowledge that the man standing before them was the prophesied Christ, surely must have seen the three days as the capstone to the foundation of their sure witness.

The sacred events of the three days unfolded in a linear fashion much like placing one building block upon another. The linear approach is most significant, for it shows a pattern of order much like the order of the seven days of Creation. Nowhere else in holy scripture is the order of the gospel—the priorities—presented with such clarity.

As you review with me the three days the resurrected Lord was in the land of Bountiful, keep in mind the linear approach leading from a foundation of witnesses to the capstone of sacred silence.

The First Day

Christ established His authority among the witnesses. After speaking to His prophet Nephi, the resurrected Lord chose from among the multitude twelve righteous men to be His disciples. It is not surprising that Nephi was the first disciple named by the Lord or that his "brother whom [Nephi] had raised from the dead" was also numbered among the twelve (3 Nephi 19:4). Six of the disciples had biblical names—Zedekiah, Isaiah, Jonas (two had that name), Jeremiah, and Timothy—and six had Nephite names—Mathoni, Mathonihah, Kumen, Kumennonhi, Shemnon, and Nephi.

The multitude had the privilege of witnessing the selection of the twelve. Such an opportunity contrasts with the Savior's selection of the Twelve Apostles in Jerusalem, which was much more of a private affair. To me, the contrast suggests the righteous state of the multitude in Bountiful compared to any multitude in Jerusalem.

After Jesus gave the twelve disciples power and authority, "he stretched forth his hand unto the multitude and cried unto them, saying: Blessed are ye if ye shall give heed unto the words of these twelve whom I have chosen from among you to minister unto you, and to be your servants" (3 Nephi 12:1). He then gave the twelve disciples power and authority to administer the ordinance of baptism. Although the disciples now had the right to baptize, they did not immediately begin to baptize. Instead, they joined the multitude and listened as the resurrected Lord spoke the words of Gospel writers Matthew, Mark, Luke, and John, the things He had taught those in Jerusalem. What stands out in the conveyance of these words is not the subject, for you and I are familiar with the gospel teachings presented in the Bible. It is the manner in which the words were delivered.

The words were presented precept upon precept, not line upon line (lines being stories). There were no parables or stories used by the resurrected Lord to illustrate doctrine. Perhaps in anticipation that His doctrine would be repeated verbatim by the twelve disciples, the resurrected Lord told the multitude, who may have been more familiar with precepts punctuated by lines, "Blessed are ye if ye shall give heed unto the words of these twelve" (3 Nephi 12:1).

Doctrine was taught. Christ's teachings that first day are compiled in three short chapters—3 Nephi 12–14. They begin with the beatitudes and end with the wise man who built his house upon a rock and the foolish man who built his house upon the sand (see 3 Nephi 14: 24–27). The Lord's summation of His teachings was, "Ye have heard the things which I taught before I ascended to my Father" (3 Nephi 15:1). In other words, all that Jesus taught in a three-year period in Jerusalem was conveyed to the Nephites on the first day of His visit with them.

How is that possible, knowing that many of His teachings are missing in 3 Nephi 12–14? I remind and console myself that Mormon abridged the record and confessed, "And now there cannot be written in this book even a hundredth part of the things which Jesus did truly teach unto the people" (3 Nephi 26:6).

After His gospel discourse, the resurrected Lord looked upon the multitude and perceived that they could not understand all the words His Father had commanded Him to speak. Did He regret not punctuating His doctrine with stories? I think not, for the exception was the sure knowledge of the twelve disciples, who would the next day teach the "same words which Jesus had spoken—nothing varying from the words which Jesus had spoken" (3 Nephi 19:8).

Perhaps in recognition that the people had grown weary, the resurrected Lord invited them to go to their homes and prepare their minds for the second day by pondering His teachings and praying to their Father in Heaven. Although the Lord's words were stronger than a mere invitation, the multitude lingered.

The power of the priesthood was shown forth. With tear-filled eyes, they steadfastly gazed upon the resurrected Lord, for they desired to be not only recipients of His teachings but recipients of His miracles (3 Nephi 17:1–5). Doesn't this sound like you and me? Do you think we would have packed up our tents and gone home?

Knowing their thoughts, the Lord said, "I see that your faith is sufficient that I should heal you" (3 Nephi 17:8). He healed the lame, the blind, the withered, and all those who were afflicted (see 3 Nephi 17:9). Would such healings not have taken longer than thrusting hands in His side or feeling the prints of the nails? It is not surprising that those who were healed of afflictions bathed the Lord's feet with their tears (see 3 Nephi 17:10).

Next was the Lord's blessing of little children. Though He had blessed children in Jerusalem, the New Testament account is painfully sparse when compared to the moving portrayal in the Americas. Can you imagine the Lord blessing each child, weeping as He did so, or the celestial fire surrounding the little ones and seeing angels descend to minister unto them? (see 3 Nephi 17:21–24).

The sacrament was administered. In Jerusalem, Jesus fed a multitude with loaves and fishes, but only to His Apostles assembled in the Upper

Room on the Feast of the Passover did He administer the bread and wine of the sacrament (see Matthew 26:26–29). In Bountiful, on the first day of His ministry, Jesus extended the blessing of partaking of the sacrament to all. He broke the bread and blessed it and gave it to his twelve disciples. They in turn blessed the sacred emblems and distributed them to the multitude (see 3 Nephi 18:3–4). "And when the multitude had eaten and were filled" (3 Nephi 18:5), it was then that the Lord made plain the sanctity and purpose of the sacrament: "It shall be a testimony unto the Father that ye do always remember me. And if ye do always remember me ye shall have my Spirit to be with you" (3 Nephi 18:7).

The power to give the gift of the Holy Ghost was conferred upon the twelve disciples. The Lord touched His disciples with His hand one by one as He spoke to them. The disciples reported that in that sacred moment, the Lord gave them "power to give the Holy Ghost" (3 Nephi 18:37). That gift was the fulfilment of a prophecy uttered by Nephi, son of Lehi—"unto all those who diligently seek him, as well in times of old as in the time that he should manifest himself unto the children of men" (1 Nephi 10:17).

Then, as if unexpected, a cloud "overshadowed the multitude that they could not see Jesus. And while they were overshadowed he departed from them, and ascended into heaven" (3 Nephi 18:38–39).

The Second Day

The covenant of baptism was instituted. Those who gathered at Bountiful the second day were not numbered. However, it is known that their number exceeded that of the first day (see 3 Nephi 19:5). If you had missed the first day, would you not have traveled through the night to be present the second day?

The second day began with messages from the twelve disciples, the only men who had witnessed the resurrected Lord ascend into heaven the first day (see 3 Nephi 19:6). Words of the disciples, repetitive of the words of the resurrected Lord, continued until Nephi walked down to "the water's edge" (3 Nephi 19:10). Wanting to observe what would take place, the multitude followed him. Nephi walked into the water and was baptized. He then baptized the disciples in obedience to the Lord's command: "I give unto you power that ye shall baptize this people when I am again ascended into heaven" (3 Nephi 19:12; 3 Nephi 11:21). After each had been baptized, "they were encircled about . . . by fire; and it came down from heaven, and the multitude did witness it, and did bear record; and angels did come down out of heaven and did minister unto them" (3 Nephi 19:14–15). It was then that Jesus was seen standing "in the midst and ministered unto them" (3 Nephi 19:15).

Christ prayed unto the Father. With the presence of the resurrected Lord came an invitation to the multitude to kneel down upon the earth and pray. The Lord did likewise but knelt away from the crowd. Kneeling in prayer, He expressed gratitude to His Father for giving His disciples the Holy Ghost and asked His Father to give the Holy Ghost to all who would believe on their words (see 3 Nephi 19:20–21). Jesus then returned to the disciples and found them engaged in prayer. Observing their faithfulness, the Lord's countenance shined upon the twelve (see 3 Nephi 19:25).

At this point, the resurrected Lord again left the disciples to pray to His Father (see 3 Nephi 19:28). This time, He asked His Father to purify His disciples and those who believe on their words because of their faith (see 3 Nephi 19:28). After concluding this prayer, He returned to the disciples and found them still steadfastly praying (see 3 Nephi 19:30). Again, He left them to pray to His Father. "Tongue cannot speak the words which he prayed, neither can be written by man the words he prayed"—however, the multitude heard His prayer and understood His words (see 3 Nephi 19:32–33). When Jesus returned to His disciples a third time and found them still in prayer, He said, "So great faith have I never seen among all the Jews" (3 Nephi 19:35).

The ordinance of sacrament was repeated. The resurrected Lord blessed the sacred emblems of the sacrament and gave them to His disciples (see 3 Nephi 20:3–6). The disciples, in turn, blessed the sacred emblems and distributed them to the multitude. What is most miraculous about this ordinance of sacrament is "there had been no bread, neither wine, brought by the disciples, neither by the multitude" (3 Nephi 20:6). After partaking of the emblems, the multitude cried with one voice, giving glory to Jesus Christ (see 3 Nephi 20:9).

The resurrected Lord read from holy scripture. The focus of the Lord's message to His disciples and the multitude on the second day was the writings of Isaiah about the building of New Jerusalem, the return of the lost tribes, and the gathering of Israel (see 3 Nephi 20:11). The Lord commanded the multitude to search the words of Isaiah, explaining that they masterfully describe the remnant of Jacob and explain how that remnant will come to a knowledge of the Lord and inherit the lands of Joseph (see 1 Nephi 20:11–13). He further told of Isaiah portraying the Gentiles as a free people in the promised land and of their being saved if they would believe and obey his words.

The Lord then moved on to the prophecies of Samuel the Lamanite (see 3 Nephi 23:9) and Malachi (see 3 Nephi 24:1). He wanted Samuel's prophecy of the Saints rising from the dead included in Nephite scripture (see 3 Nephi 23:9). From the words of Malachi, the Lord wanted the assemblage to know that a messenger would prepare the way for His Second Coming, even the Second Coming of Jesus Christ (see 3 Nephi 24). This was not all, for the Lord "did expound all things, even from the beginning until the time that he should come in his glory" (3 Nephi 26:3). He then ascended into heaven.

The Third Day

The third day is perhaps the most intriguing of the Lord's ministry, for it raises more questions than answers. For example, it is not known how the Lord descended to the land of Bountiful on the third day. On the first day, He descended from heaven; on the second day, He was seen among the twelve. What of the third day? Furthermore, it is not known what He taught on the third day. On the first day, He expanded and clarified teachings recorded by Gospel writers Matthew, Mark, Luke, and John. On the second day, the subject of His gospel discourse was taken from ancient prophets. What new words did He have on the third day? (see 3 Nephi 26:16).

Mormon is all but silent about the third day of the resurrected Lord's ministry with the exception of a generality: "The Lord truly did teach the people, for the space of three days; and after that he did show himself unto them oft, and did break bread oft, and bless it, and give it unto them" (3 Nephi 26:13).

Although I lament the "sacred silence"—the capstone—that shrouds the third day, I take joy in what is known of the resurrected Lord's ministry in the Western hemisphere. Where else in holy scripture can you find a more blessed multitude than the one gathered near the temple in Bountiful in AD 34? Where else can you read of such a glorious appearance of the resurrected Lord, His clarity of teaching, and of multiple miracles in such a short period of time?

Yet the Western hemisphere ministry of the resurrected Lord was not confined to three days. Mormon writes that the Lord did "show himself unto them oft, and did break bread oft, and bless it, and give it unto them" (3 Nephi 26:13). But before the year AD 34 had ended, it was the "disciples whom Jesus had chosen," not the Lord, who were teaching and ministering to the people (3 Nephi 26:17). It was the disciples who healed the sick and the infirm and raised the dead in the name of Jesus Christ (see 4 Nephi 1:5).

As the Nephites listened and embraced the words of the disciples and the words of those who had witnessed the resurrected Lord in the land of Bountiful, a period of profound love flooded the hearts of their generation and generations that followed. For 150 years, the love of God dwelt within every heart. All people acted justly with each other and prospered and multiplied. They lived in peace and harmony as a purified people, united in their knowledge and understanding of Jesus Christ.

"And they had all things common among them; therefore there were not rich and poor . . . and the Lord did prosper them exceedingly in the land" (4 Nephi 1:3, 7). This prosperity led to the scriptural observation, "Surely there could not be a happier people among all the people who had been created by the hand of God" (4 Nephi 1:16).

Gone were the days when opposition in all things dominated their culture—centuries in which the majority of ancient Americans rejected the word of God and set a methodical course for spiritual failure. Echoes of such deviants as King Noah and Nehor held no sway in the hearts and minds of the people after the ascension of the resurrected Lord. Love of riches, rebellion against God, and enticements of Satan that brought a sense of trepidation and solemn foreboding, even forewarning of the wrath of God to come, were historical remembrances but not topics that dominated their lives. It was a time when the Lord did not send a righteous exemplar for every apostate as had been the case for generations—for a Korihor, an Alma; for a Sherem, a Jacob; and for an Amalickiah, a Captain Moroni. It was a peaceful time when evil speaking of the Lord's anointed was erased.

The cry of repentance and the problems associated with choosing the broad path to spiritual and material ruin or preaching about blessings that come from choosing the narrow path, the iron rod that leads to spiritual well-being, was not necessary. Failure and its recurring ills was a product of yesteryear, when the choice to not keep the commandments of God was the norm. What one word best describes generations of Nephites for 150 years? They were *Christlike*, for the Nephites were purified in their knowledge and understanding of Jesus Christ. They were firm and steadfast in their hope that one day they would again see their Savior and know the joy that surpasses earthly understanding as they returned to their Father in Heaven.

CHAPTER NINE
MIRACLES AND THE BELIEVERS

And that he manifesteth himself unto all those who believe . . .
working mighty miracles, signs, and wonders,
among the children of men according to their faith.
(2 Nephi 26:13)

In his October 2018 general conference address, President Russell M. Nelson advised the sisters to "be intentional about talking of Christ, rejoicing in Christ, and preaching of Christ with your family and friends." He promised that by doing so, "You and they will be drawn closer to the Savior through this process. And changes, even miracles, will begin to happen."[36] That advice and promise are not new. Ancient prophets of the Book of Mormon also counseled their followers to talk of Christ, rejoice in Christ, and preach of Christ. The result of such a Christ-centered life was the attendant blessing of miracles.

Don't let the fact that most ancient Americans rejected the word of God lead you to conclude that miracles were few in the lives of the faithful. Don't be so caught up in the stories of King Noah, Gadianton, Nehor, and the masses who rebelled against God that you miss the sacred. Let us look together at the miracles that naturally followed the ancient inhabitants of the Western hemisphere who talked of Christ, rejoiced in Christ, and preached of Christ.

The Book of Mormon is filled with messages of hope for the righteous minority who hearkened to the words of holy prophets, stayed on the narrow path, and clung to the iron rod that led to a Christ-centered life. Just as there were prophets and Saints in ancient America, there are prophets and Saints today who choose the less-trodden path.

---

[36] Nelson, "Sisters' Participation in the Gathering of Israel."

Take my Sunday School class for example—Virginia, a mentally challenged young girl, asked, "Can I sing 'The First Noel'?" Although the Christmas season was half a year away and the Christmas carol had little to do with the lesson, I nodded my head in approval. Virginia smiled and laughed before standing up and facing the class. She then sang from memory five stanzas of "The First Noel" before an awkward silence evidenced she could not recall the next stanza. Before I could step in and help, Virginia was crying. Without prompting, a child in class started singing "The First Noel" from the beginning. Virginia smiled and joined her, as did the other children. When they finished, Virginia asked, "Do you want to sing 'Silent Night' with me?" They did.

The planned lesson was never given, for that day, in a small classroom of a ward meetinghouse, a little girl, despondent and despairing, was made glad by the Christlike actions of her friends. When class ended and the children walked out into the hall, Virginia was not walking alone. One child held Virginia's hand, another carried her scriptures, and yet another announced to her mother, "Virginia sang 'The First Noel.' She's awesome." These children quietly lifted the burden of an unhappy child—a child that some incorrectly assumed was the least among them.

To me, the children that day were like Nephi, Helaman, Alma, and a host of faithful Saints of yesteryear who stepped forward and did the right thing. But I wondered as they left the classroom if their choice would be the same when they grew to maturity. There would be other Virginias needing comfort. Would they be uncaring, or would they pause from their crowded lives to help? The answer to my musings has little to do with the Virginias in their lives. It has everything to do with a conviction that Jesus is the Christ.

"Believest thou in Jesus Christ, who shall come?" Alma asked Helaman. "And he said: Yea, I believe all the words which thou hast spoken" (Alma 45:4–5). In more than one respect, Helaman's response represents that of the faithful Saints in the Western hemisphere and Saints today. Helaman was like thousands of Lamanites who never faltered in their testimony of Christ (see Alma 23:6). He was like the stripling warriors whose faith in God was so strong that "not one soul of them [did fall] to the earth" as they fought for the cause of liberty (Alma 56:56). I am convinced that Helaman, like an earlier prophet, Jacob, could have written, "We did magnify our office unto the Lord, taking upon us the responsibility" of teaching the word of God and the need for repentance to the people (Jacob 1:19; Jacob 2:2).

Yet Helaman, like other ancient American prophets, was not immune from suffering and persecution. Where was the miracle that followed his rejoicing and preaching of Christ? In the Jaredite culture, those who listened to holy men were cast out; some were thrown into pits and left to perish (see Ether 9:29). In the Nephite culture, those who listened to prophets and testified boldly of Christ were "taken and put to death secretly by the judges" (3 Nephi 6:23). Alma and Amulek were forced to witness women and children being cast into a fire because of their belief in Jesus Christ (see Alma 14:8–9). How can I explain such suffering when I know that miracles follow those who believe in Christ?

The miracles presented in the Book of Mormon are written for us to discover. For example, is it not a miracle that the same Alma, who witnessed women and children being cast into the fire for their belief in Christ, exclaimed, "O that I were an angel, and could have the wish of mine heart, that I might go forth and speak with the trump of God, with a voice to shake the earth, and cry repentance unto every people!" (Alma 29:1). Is it not a miracle that Ether "did cry from the morning, even until the going down of the sun, exhorting the people to believe in God unto repentance" when he had to hide in a cave from his enemies? (Ether 12:3).

Rather than back down from preaching of Christ and accepting a more modulated, wishy-washy approach to the gospel, Nephi said to his accusers, "O ye fools, ye uncircumcised of heart, ye blind, and ye stiffnecked people" (Helaman 9:21). Samuel the Lamanite shouted from the walls of the Nephite city of Zarahemla, "O ye wicked and ye perverse generation; ye hardened and ye stiffnecked people, how long will ye suppose that the Lord will suffer you?" (Helaman 13:29).

Although the meaning of their cry was clear, the reception of their cry was mixed. The prophetic cry caused multitudes to fall to their knees (see Helaman 6:4–6). Most often, the cry was muffled, if not stamped out, by the flagrant vices of the people (see Helaman 7:3; Ether 13:2, 13). This did not stop the prophets from proclaiming the word of God. They remained steadfast in their declarations, for they knew that repentance was essential to salvation and that without it no accountable person could be saved in the kingdom of God (see Mosiah 17:10–11). They wanted their generation to know the freedom that comes from casting off the burden of guilt and becoming clean from sin.

But when their message was rebuffed, there were no borders to contain their sorrow. Nephi grieved greatly because of the hardness of his brothers' hearts (see 1 Nephi 7:8). Jacob confessed, "I this day am weighed down with much more desire and anxiety for the welfare of your souls than I have hitherto been" (Jacob 2:3). Mormon cried, "And woe is me because of their wickedness; for my heart has been filled with sorrow because of their wickedness, all my days" (Mormon 2:19). Even the three disciples who tarried on the earth after the ascension of the resurrected Lord "sorrow[ed] for the sins of the world" (4 Nephi 1:44). Where were their miracles?

Instead of experiencing a miracle, often their sorrow grew in intensity as the prophets became the target of unbridled persecution. From 600 BC, when the people of Jerusalem sought to take Lehi's life (see 1 Nephi 1:19–20), to AD 421, when Moroni faced destruction by the Lamanites (see Moroni 1:1), persecution was the lot and heritage of prophets. Like Christ, who endured scourging, mockery, thorns, and death, His prophets and His Saints endured persecution. Nephi fled from his plotting brothers (see 2 Nephi 5:1–6). Alma and Amulek endured prison (see Alma 14:22). Ether dwelt in the cavity of a rock (see Ether 13:18). And Abinadi suffered death by fire (see Mosiah 17:20).

Knowing that persecution, even death, followed their preaching, the question is still—*Where is the miracle?* After all, these holy prophets talked of Christ, preached of Christ, and rejoiced in Christ.

May I suggest that the obvious, if not the first, miracle in the lives of the faithful was their unshakable testimony of Jesus Christ. The prophets would not and did not deny their testimony of Christ. For example, Abinadi said, "I will not recall the words which I have spoken unto you concerning this people, for they are true; and that ye may know of their surety I have suffered myself that I have fallen into your hands. Yea, and I will suffer even until death, and I will not recall my words, and they shall stand as a testimony against you" (Mosiah 17:9–10).

To me, never did the prophets stand taller than when they testified of Christ in the face of persecution. Instead of renouncing God for his suffering, Nephi rejoiced and expressed the sure knowledge that "the Lord hath redeemed my soul from hell; I have beheld his glory, and I am encircled about eternally in the arms of his love" (2 Nephi 1:15). Enos wrote, "I soon go to the place of my rest, which is with my Redeemer; for I know that in him I shall rest" (Enos 1:27). Alma affirmed, "I know that he will raise me up at the last day, to dwell with him in glory" (Alma 36:28).

The way I see it, these holy men "press[ed] forward with a steadfastness in Christ, having a perfect brightness of hope, and a love of God and of all men." They "feast[ed] upon the word of Christ, and endure[d] to the end." To them, the Father surely said, "Ye shall have eternal life" (2 Nephi 31:20).

As they endured persecution, mockery, and blatant hatred, one truth becomes poignantly clear: miracles occurred in each of their lives. The miracle came in the form of heavenly comfort and strength. Just as God the Father comforted his Beloved Son, so he comforted His prophets in times of need. Although the prophets must have known that the pathway of godly sorrow leads to eternal glory, that persecution for righteousness' sake leads to the kingdom of heaven, and that heavenly strength given in times of trial is a foreshadow of eternity's power, they now knew these truths on a personal level.

The Book of Mormon reveals the following miracles in the lives of ancient prophets:

The Lord sent angels to minister to His prophets. An angel intervened when Nephi was smitten by a rod at the hands of his elder brothers (see 1 Nephi 3:28–30). Angels ministered to Jacob when he contended with Sherem about the truthfulness of Christ (see Jacob 7:5). When Alma was "weighed down with sorrow, wading through much tribulation and anguish of soul, because of the wickedness of the people . . . an angel of the Lord appeared unto him, saying: Blessed art thou, Alma" (Alma 8:14–15). When Lehi and Nephi were in prison, they "were encircled about as if by fire" (Helaman 5:23), and they conversed with the angels of God (see Helaman 5:39). In the case of a dejected Nephi, "angels did minister unto him daily" (3 Nephi 7:18).

The Lord delivered His prophets from persecution. Mosiah was warned by the Lord to flee out of the land of Nephi (see Omni 1:12). The Lord delivered Abinadi from his enemies when his life was threatened (see Mosiah 11:26). Alma and Amulek could not be confined in dungeons or slain, for the Lord delivered them from their enemies (see Alma 8:31; Alma 14:26–27; Alma 36:27). Helaman was astonished that his two thousand stripling warriors were spared from the grasp of death (see Alma 58:39). Nephi was "taken by the Spirit and conveyed away out of the midst" of his enemies (see Helaman 10:16).

The Lord preserved His prophets as they faced persecution. Nephi wrote, "My God hath been my support; he hath led me through mine afflictions in the wilderness; and he hath preserved me upon the waters of the great deep" (2 Nephi 4:20). The Lord preserved Abinadi when the king wanted him slain (see Mosiah 13:3). The Lord strengthened the people of Alma "that they could bear up their burdens with ease, and they did submit cheerfully and with patience to all the will of the Lord" (Mosiah 24:15).

The Lord watched over His servants as they preached among the apostate Zoramites (see Alma 31:38). Samuel the Lamanite was not hit by stones or arrows as he stood on the wall of Zarahemla due to the preserving power of God (see Helaman 16:2).

Someday we will meet these ancient prophets before the bar of God. "You and I shall stand face to face before his bar," wrote Nephi (2 Nephi 33:11). Jacob bade us farewell "until I shall meet you before the pleasing bar of God" (Jacob 6:13). And Moroni penned, "Ye shall see me at the bar of God" (Moroni 10:27). When we meet these holy men, will we tell of the promises made by President Nelson in October 2018 that by reading their words, we would "be drawn closer to the Savior" and of the "changes, even miracles" in our own lives, or will we speak of less-than-casual interest in their testimony of Christ?[37]

Perhaps it is a topic and a decision for another day. But when you find yourself halting between two opinions regarding the words of Christ, or feel indecisive like Alice in Lewis Carroll's classic *Alice's Adventures in Wonderland*, may I suggest that you follow the admonition of President Thomas S. Monson:

> You will remember that [Alice] comes to a crossroads with two paths before her, each stretching onward but in opposite directions. She is confronted by the Cheshire cat, of whom Alice asks, "Which path shall I follow?" The cat answers, "That depends where you want to go. If you do not know where you want to go, it doesn't matter which path you take."
>
> Unlike Alice, we all know where we want to go, and it *does* matter which way we go, for by choosing our path, we choose our destination.[38]

Putting it another way to drive home the point, consider the children's hymn, "I Am a Child of God."[39] When the lyrics of the hymn were written by composer Naomi Randall, one phrase read, "Teach me all that I must *know* | To live with Him someday" (emphasis added). The phrase suggests that knowledge is all that is needed to live with God

---

[37] Ibid.

[38] Thomas S. Monson, "The Three Rs of Choice," *Ensign*, November 2010.

[39] "I Am a Child of God," *Hymns of The Church of Jesus Christ of Latter-day Saints* (Salt Lake City: The Church of Jesus Christ of Latter-day Saints, 1985), 301.

again. To the Latter-day Saint who hopes that making mental note of the encyclopedic minutia of the gospel will result in living "with Him someday," here's the bad news—knowledge is not enough.

The phrase "Teach me all that I must *know* | To live with him someday" was changed by President Spencer W. Kimball. President Kimball said in reference to the composer, "Naomi Randall wrote most of the words, but I wrote one!"[40] President Kimball changed one word—"Teach me all that I must *do* | To live with him someday" (emphasis added). "Do it" and "Lengthen your stride" became catchphrases of President Kimball's administration.

Attempting to match knowledge with actions comes easy for some. They recognize that it is not enough to define faith; faithful actions are needed to obtain salvation. It is not just enough to define modesty, morality, or honesty—action is needed to make hope an eternal reality.

Now that I have discovered the miracles that come from rejoicing and preaching of Christ as presented in the Book of Mormon, I am led to imagine another change in the lyrics: "Teach me all that I must *be* | To live with Him someday" (emphasis added). A form of the verb *to be* is "I am." When Jehovah appeared to Moses on Mount Sinai, Moses asked Him, "Behold, when I come unto the children of Israel, and shall say unto them, The God of your fathers hath sent me unto you; and they shall say to me, What is his name? what shall I say unto them? And God said unto Moses, I AM THAT I AM" (Exodus 3:13–14).

Is it really enough to know or to do? *To be* is to be as Christ is—Christlike. *To be* is the quest, or as Shakespeare's leading character Hamlet said, "To be, or not to be, that is the question."[41]

---

[40] Karen Lynn Davidson, *Our Latter-day Hymns: The Stories and the Messages* (Salt Lake City: Deseret Book, 1998), 303–304; "New Verse Is Written for Popular Song," *Church News*, April 1, 1978.

[41] William Shakespeare, *Hamlet*, act III, scene I, line 64.

CHAPTER TEN
A TYPE AND SHADOW OF ANCIENT PROPHETS

*For I am the Lord thy God, and will be with thee even unto
the end of the world, and through all eternity; for verily I seal upon you
your exaltation, and prepare a throne for you
in the kingdom of my Father, with Abraham your father.
(D&C 132:49)*

As is the pattern for all prophets of old, the life and words of Joseph Smith teach us how to be as Christ is. Joseph's life reveals a parallel course with the lives of ancient prophets in the Western hemisphere.

While yet in his youth, Joseph Smith was privileged to see Jesus Christ. Like the twenty-two men named in the Book of Mormon who saw Christ, Joseph left his testimony of the Savior's appearance to him:

> It was on the morning of a beautiful, clear day, early in the spring of eighteen hundred and twenty.... I saw a pillar of light exactly over my head, above the brightness of the sun, which descended gradually until it fell upon me.... When the light rested upon me I saw two Personages, whose brightness and glory defy all description, standing above me in the air. One of them spake unto me, calling me by name and said, pointing to the other—*This is My Beloved Son, Hear Him!*" (Joseph Smith—History 1:14–17)

Joseph also left his testimony of the coming forth of the Book of Mormon. On September 21, 1823, as Joseph lay in bed, he "discovered a light appearing in my room, which continued to increase until the room was lighter than at noonday, when immediately a personage appeared at my bedside, standing in the air, for his feet did not touch the floor" (Joseph Smith—History 1:30). The angelic personage "called me by name, and said unto me that he was a messenger sent from the presence of God to me, and that his name was Moroni" (Joseph Smith—History 1:33).

From Moroni, Joseph learned that "God had a work for me to do; and that my name should be had for good and evil among all nations, kindreds, and tongues, or that it should be both good and evil spoken of among all people" (Joseph Smith—History 1:33). He was told of a book written on plates that had the appearance of gold and of the Urim and Thummim that had been prepared to help him translate the plates. As angel Moroni spoke of these sacred things, "the place [the hill] where the plates were deposited" was shown to Joseph in vision (Joseph Smith—History 1:42). When the illuminating scene ended, the angel departed. Before dawn, however, the angelic messenger reappeared again and again until his visits "occupied the whole of that night" (Joseph Smith—History 1:47).

The next morning, Joseph arose from his bed with plans to go about the "necessary labors of the day" (Joseph Smith—History 1:48). He went to the fields, but in so doing he discovered that his strength was gone. He started to return to his family home, but as he did so, his steps were arrested. The angel again appeared and "related unto me all that he had related to me the previous night, and commanded me to go to my father and tell him of the vision and commandments which I had received" (Joseph Smith—History 1:49). In compliance with the angelic instructions, Joseph retraced his steps to the field and told his father of the angel and his message. "It was of God," affirmed Joseph Smith Sr. (Joseph Smith—History 1:50).

Joseph went to the place shown him in vision—"a hill of considerable size, and the most elevated of any in the neighborhood" (Joseph Smith—History 1:51). There on the hill, he discovered "under a stone of considerable size, lay the plates, deposited in a stone box" (Joseph Smith—History 1:51). He attempted to remove the plates from the receptacle but was prevented by the same heavenly messenger. "The time for bringing them forth had not yet arrived," Joseph was told, and it would not arrive "until he had learned to keep the commandments of God—not only till he was willing but able to do it" (Joseph Smith—History 1:53).[42]

Four years passed before twenty-one-year-old Joseph Smith was given the plates and the Urim and Thummim. During that interim,

---

[42] "Lucy Mack Smith, History, 1844–1845, 85," *The Joseph Smith Papers*.

he would describe the ancient inhabitants of this continent their dress their manner of traveling the animals which they rode The cities that were built by them the structure of their buildings with every particular of their mode of warfare their religious worship as particularly as though he had Spent his life with them.[43]

His brother William Smith was asked, "Did you not doubt Joseph's testimony sometimes?"

William replied, "No . . . we all had the most implicit confidence in what he said. He was a truthful boy. Father and Mother believed him, why should not the children?"[44]

The Smith family was "confirmed in the opinion that God was about to bring to light something upon which we could stay our minds, or that would give us a more perfect knowledge of the plan of salvation and the redemption of the human family." Their conviction of forthcoming truth led Joseph's mother, Lucy Mack Smith, to pen, "Tranquility reigned in our midst."[45]

When Joseph received the golden plates on September 27, 1827, "with this charge: that I should be responsible for them; that if I should let them go carelessly, or through any neglect of mine, I should be cut off," it was not an idle threat (Joseph Smith—History 1:59). "Satan had now stirred up the hearts of those who had gotten a hint of the matter," wrote Joseph, "to search into it and make every possible move towards thwarting the purposes of the Almighty." Mobs shouted, "We will have the plates in spite of Joe Smith or all the Devils in Hell."[46] Knowing their determination, Joseph hid the plates in sundry places around the family farm, hoping to keep thieves at bay.

Instead of being frustrated by his tactics, the would-be thieves grew more vigilant in their efforts. To keep the plates safe, Joseph and his wife, Emma, found it best to leave Palmyra. For a time, they lived at the home of Emma's father, Isaac Hale, in Harmony, Pennsylvania. The Hale home provided a brief respite until Father Hale discovered Joseph had secret

---

[43] "Lucy Mack Smith, History, 1844-1845, Page [1–2], bk. 4," p. [1-2], bk. 4, *The Joseph Smith Papers*.

[44] J. W. Peterson, "William B. Smith's Last Statement," *Zion's Ensign* 5, no. 3 (1894), 6.

[45] "Lucy Mack Smith History, 1844–1845, Page [1], bk. 4," *The Joseph Smith Papers*.

[46] "Lucy Mack Smith, History, 1844–1845, Page 9, Book 5," *The Joseph Smith Papers*.

contents that he could not see. Joseph and Emma then sought a home of their own in Harmony. In their own abode, a son was born—who died a few hours after his birth—and the book of Lehi was translated, only to have the manuscript of the book stolen or misplaced.

After these losses, there came a sense of peace into Joseph Smith's home—a blessing associated with translating and scribing the Book of Mormon. His wife, Emma, recalled, "I am satisfied that no man could have dictated the writing of the manuscripts unless he was inspired." Explaining the process, Emma continued, "When acting as his scribe, [he] would dictate to me hour after hour; and when returning after meals, or after interruptions, he would at once begin where he had left off, without either seeing the manuscript or having any portion of it read to him." As Emma affirmed, "This was a usual thing for him to do. It would have been improbable that a learned man could do this; and, for one so ignorant and unlearned as he was, it was simply impossible."47 Scribe Oliver Cowdery added, "These were days never to be forgotten—to sit under the sound of a voice dictated by the *inspiration* of heaven, awakened the utmost gratitude of this bosom. . . . to write from his mouth, as he translated, with the *Urim* and *Thummim* . . . the history, or record, called 'The book of Mormon.'"48

Like the prophets of ancient America, Joseph Smith gathered around him a multitude who knew by faith, not by sight, that Jesus was the Christ. The multitude also knew that the Book of Mormon was the word of God to their generation. Many remained true to their testimonies of Christ and the Book of Mormon in spite of adverse circumstances, such as the Battle of Crooked River, a government-sanctioned extermination order, and the Hawn's Mill Massacre.

As for Joseph Smith, he never wavered in his testimony. Like the ancient prophets in the Western hemisphere, Joseph magnified his calling as a prophet, seer, and revelator. He did not shrink from the responsibility to prophesy (D&C 21:5) or to cry repentance (D&C 6:9). The Doctrine and Covenants is filled with Joseph's prophecies pertaining to the past, the present, and the future (see D&C 1:37–39; 11:25; 21:4–5; Articles of Faith 1:7). Likewise, the Doctrine and Covenants is a repository of Joseph's cry of repentance (see D&C 1:27; 6:9; 11:9; 16:6; 42:24–28; 133:16).

---

[47] "Last Testimony of Sister Emma," *The Saints' Herald*, vol. 26 (October 1, 1879), 290.
[48] *Latter-day Saints' Messenger and Advocate*, vol. 1, no. 1 (October 1834), 14.

Like the cry of ancient prophets, most of Joseph's words were rejected by his generation. Rejection was followed by persecution. Ridicule, arrest warrants, and evil speaking were Joseph's common foes. Enemies, mobs, and traitors sought to thwart his every move. Doctrines Joseph held sacred—such as plural marriage, temple ordinances, and the nature of God—were distorted by apostates to disprove his claims of divine revelation and to arouse public sentiment against him. It is not a stretch to say that persecution stalked him from the spring of 1820 to his martyrdom in June 1844.

Yet amid the persecution, suffering, rejection, and loneliness, the Lord did not leave Joseph comfortless. Like the prophets of the Book of Mormon, Joseph was comforted and strengthened by the Lord in his extremities. Joseph conversed with angels (see Joseph Smith—History 1:30). While in Liberty Jail under the sentence of death, the Lord promised deliverance and that Joseph's friends would greet him again "with warm hearts and friendly hands" (D&C 121:9). Joseph spoke to fellow prisoners of his confidence in the Lord's preserving power: "Be of good cheer, brethren; the word of the Lord came to me last night that our lives should be given us, and that whatever we may suffer during this captivity, not one of our lives should be taken."[49] Joseph and his associates were spared, as prophesied.

It was not until June 27, 1844, that Joseph's life was taken at Carthage, Illinois. For Joseph, Carthage was a scene of broken promises, oaths of conspiracy, illegal arraignment, and fatal incarceration. Fallacious rumors, once whispered, were shouted as throngs unabashedly declared that Joseph would not leave Carthage alive. A Warsaw mob sang, "Where now is the Prophet Joseph? Where now is the Prophet Joseph? Where now is the Prophet Joseph? Safe in Carthage jail!"[50] Even the governor of Illinois, though not in boisterous song, joined with the chorus of conspirators and militia in abetting the deaths of Joseph and his brother Hyrum.

Unwittingly, the assassins left behind much more than the corpses of two men. They left "a broad seal affixed to 'Mormonism' that cannot be rejected by any court on earth" (D&C 135:7). They left "truth of the everlasting gospel that all the world cannot impeach" (D&C 135:7). They

---

[49] Joseph Smith quote as stated by Parley P. Pratt, *Autobiography of Parley Parker Pratt*, 210.
[50] Introduction to Administrative Records, Volume 1, *The Joseph Smith Papers*; B. H. Roberts, *A Comprehensive History of The Church of Jesus Christ of Latter-day Saints*, 2:281.

left two martyr's crowns, which they helped forge with their senseless brutality. The testifiers are dead; yet their testament lives on. Joseph's seal is affixed to the truthfulness of the Book of Mormon. Throughout eternity, Joseph will be numbered with the sanctified and the religious martyrs of all ages.

Without equivocation, it can be said that Joseph Smith was a prophet of God who, like Nephi, Jacob, and Moroni, saw Jesus Christ. He, like Alma and Lehi, prophesied the words of God and cried repentance to his generation. As Mormon and Ether were persecuted for their testimony of the Lord, so too was Joseph. As Abinadi suffered a martyr's fate, so too did Joseph. Like Jacob, Moroni, and Nephi, Joseph knew his standing before God: "For I am the Lord thy God, and will be with thee even unto the end of the world, and through all eternity; for verily I seal upon you your exaltation, and prepare a throne for you in the kingdom of my Father, with Abraham your father" (D&C 132:49).

CHAPTER ELEVEN
A TESTIMONY TO SHARE

*I told the brethren that the Book of Mormon was
the most correct of any book on earth,
and the keystone of our religion.
—Joseph Smith*[51]

AT THIS POINT IN YOUR reading, you know that the Book of Mormon writers wrote primarily about our Savior. They mentioned some form of His name on an average of every 1.7 verses. They referred to Jesus Christ by literally 101 different names, from the first reference to Him as "Lord" in 1 Nephi 1:1 to the final name in the Book of Mormon given Him as "Eternal Judge" in Moroni 10:34. Each of the 101 names signifies a different attribute or characteristic of Jesus Christ and was used appropriately to convey recognition of who He is and what His mission represents. You also know that the central message of Christ in the Book of Mormon is the Atonement and that holy prophets in the Western hemisphere knew of, spoke of, and wrote of Christ, but only a few saw Him. The exception was in AD 34, when thousands of ancient American inhabitants saw, heard, and touched the resurrected Lord.

You may even now be testifying that the Lord's attributes of love are recorded 211 times, while the judgmental attributes of God are recorded 99 times. Perhaps you are telling family and friends that this enumeration illustrates that the Lord shows forth doubly (two to one) love for His children, even though most reject Him. Perhaps the striking similarities between the testimony and persecution of prophets in the Book of Mormon and that of Joseph Smith has given you pause.

You may have begun your own study of Jesus Christ in the Book of Mormon and "mark[ed] each verse that speaks of or refers to the Savior."

---
[51] Joseph Smith, Introduction, Book of Mormon.

No doubt you have "drawn closer to the Savior" and bear testimony of the "changes, even miracles" happening in your life.[52] No doubt, part of the miracle is that you have become a witness of truth.

To be a witness of eternal truth requires an element of faith. Take, for instance, the Book of Mormon. The most profound witness of that book was the Lord Jesus Christ, who said, "[Joseph Smith] has translated the book, even that part which I have commanded him, and as your Lord and your God liveth it is true" (D&C 17:6). Joseph Smith, the translator of the Book of Mormon, is also a witness. He told "the brethren that the Book of Mormon was the most correct of any book on earth, and the keystone of our religion, and a man would get nearer to God by abiding by its precepts, than by any other book."[53]

Then there are the Three Witnesses who were shown the golden plates by an angel. The circumstances leading up to their witness has been preserved in historic detail. It begins within the small confines of the Peter Whitmer home in Fayette, New York, in June 1829 when Oliver Cowdery, David Whitmer, and Martin Harris asked Joseph Smith to "inquire of the Lord" if they might be the designated witnesses of the golden plates. Joseph wrote, "They became so very solicitous, and teased me so much, that at length I complied, and through the Urim and Thummim" received an answer: "In addition to your testimony, the testimony of three of my servants, whom I shall call and ordain, unto whom I will show these things" (D&C 5:11).[54]

The next morning, the worship services, namely "reading, singing, and praying," took place in the Whitmer home. During the services Joseph declared, "Martin Harris . . . you have got to humble yourself before your God this day and obtain if possible a forgiveness of your sins and if you will do this it is his will that you, Oliver Cowdery and David Whitmer should look upon the plates."[55]

As the morning progressed, Joseph, Oliver, David, and Martin walked into the nearby woods to "obtain by fervent and humble prayer, the fulfillment of the promises given"—that of viewing the plates. After they kneeled down on the ground, Joseph prayed vocally to God. He was followed by the others in succession, yet they did not receive a

---

[52] Nelson, "Sisters' Participation in the Gathering of Israel."
[53] Joseph Smith quote, Introduction, Book of Mormon.
[54] "History, 1838–1856, volume A-1 [23 December 1805–30 August 1834]," *The Joseph Smith Papers*.
[55] "Lucy Mack Smith, History, 1844–1845, Page [11], bk 8," p. [11], bk. 8, *The Joseph Smith Papers*.

"manifestation of the divine favor." Believing it still possible to receive the desired answer, they "again observed the same order of prayer each calling on, and praying fervently to God in rotation."[56] The result was as before.

After the second failure, Martin Harris "proposed that he should withdraw himself from [the others], believing as he expressed himself that his presence was the cause of our not obtaining what we wished for." Accordingly, he walked away. Joseph, Oliver, and David "knelt down again, and had not been many minutes engaged in prayer" when an angel appeared and showed them the plates.[57] There were now two witnesses, but what of the third? Joseph wrote of his desire for Martin to be a witness also:

> I now left David and Oliver, and went in pursuit of Martin Harris, who I found at a considerable distance, fervently engaged in prayer, he soon told me however that he had not yet prevailed with the Lord, and earnestly requested me to join him in prayer, that he also might realize the same blessings which we had just received. We accordingly joined in prayer, and ultimately obtained our desires, for before we had yet finished, the same vision was opened to our view; at least it was again opened to me, and I once more beheld, and heard the same things; whilst at the same moment, Martin Harris cried out, apparently in an ecstasy of joy, "Tis enough; mine eyes have beheld," and jumping up he shouted, hosannah, blessing God, and otherwise rejoiced exceedingly.[58]

The Three Witnesses later wrote their testimony, which is printed in each copy of the Book of Mormon.

In addition to the testimony of the Three Witnesses is the testimony of Eight Witnesses. Near the Smith log home in Palmyra, New York, eight men retired "to a little grove where it was customary for the [Smith]

---

[56] Joseph Smith, "History of Joseph Smith," *Times and Seasons 3*, no. 21 (1 September 1842), 897–898.
[57] Ibid.; Report of an Interview with Martin Harris in January 1859 in "Mormonism—No. II," *Tiffany's Monthly 5*, no. 1 (August 1859), 166; Interview of David Whitmer in "Report of Elders Orson Pratt and Joseph F. Smith," *Deseret Evening News*, November 16, 1878.
[58] "History of Joseph Smith."

family to offer up their secret prayers." There Joseph showed the plates to the eight men, who were invited to handle the plates and to observe "the engravings thereon."[59] Their testimony is also printed in each copy of the Book of Mormon.

There is also the testimony of presidents of The Church of Jesus Christ of Latter-day Saints. Their uncompromising testimonies of the truthfulness of the Book of Mormon have greatly strengthened mine:

Brigham Young (1801–1877). "When the book of Mormon was first printed, it came to my hands in two or three weeks afterwards. . . . I examined the matter studiously for two years before I made up my mind to receive that book. I knew it was true, as well as I knew that I could see with my eyes, or feel by the touch of my fingers, or be sensible of the demonstration of any sense. Had not this been the case, I never would have embraced it to this day."[60]

John Taylor (1808–1887). "The Gospel in the Book of Mormon and the Gospel in the Bible both agree: the doctrines in both books are one. The historical part differs only: the one gives the history of an Asiatic, the other of an American people. . . . it is true, and we know it."[61]

Wilford Woodruff (1807–1898). "As I [began to read the Book of Mormon] the spirit bore witness that the record which it contained was true. I opened my eyes to see, my ears to hear, and my heart to understand. I also opened my doors to entertain the servants of God."[62]

Lorenzo Snow (1814–1901). "I know Joseph Smith to have been an honest man, a man of truth, honor, and fidelity, willing to sacrifice everything he possessed, even life itself, as a testimony to the heavens and the world that he had borne the truth to the human family. . . .

Joseph Smith declared that an angel from heaven revealed to him the golden plates of the Book of Mormon."[63]

---

[59] "Lucy Mack Smith, History, 1844–1845, Page [1], bk. 9," *The Joseph Smith Papers.*

[60] Brigham Young, "The Gospel of Salvation—A Vision—Redemption of the Earth and All that Pertains to It," *Journal of Discourses,* 26 vols. (Liverpool: Latter-Day Saints' Book Depot, 1856), 3:91.

[61] John Taylor, "Communism—Sectarianism—The Gospel and Its Effects, etc.," *Journal of Discourses,* 5:240–242.

[62] Matthias F. Cowley, *Wilford Woodruff, History of His Life and Labors* (Salt Lake City: Bookcraft, 1964), 34.

[63] Clyde J. Williams, comp., *The Teachings of Lorenzo Snow: Fifth President of the Church of Jesus Christ of Latter-day Saints* (Salt Lake City: Bookcraft, 1984), 57.

Joseph F. Smith (1838–1918). "[The Book of Mormon] cannot be disproved, for it is true. There is not a word of doctrine, of admonition, of instruction within its lids, but what agrees in sentiment and veracity with those of Christ and His Apostles, as contained in the Bible. Neither is there a word of counsel, of admonition or reproof within its lids, but what is calculated to make a bad man a good man, and a good man a better man, if he will hearken to it. It bears the mark of inspiration from beginning to end, and carries conviction to every honest-hearted soul."[64]

Heber J. Grant (1856–1945). "The Book of Mormon is in absolute harmony from start to finish with other sacred scriptures. There is not a doctrine taught in it that does not harmonize with the teachings of Jesus Christ. There is not one single expression in the Book of Mormon that would wound in the slightest degree the sensitiveness of any individual. There is not a thing in it but what is for the benefit and uplift of mankind. It is in every way a true witness for God, and it sustains the Bible and is in harmony with the Bible."[65]

George Albert Smith (1870–1951). "It fills my heart with joy to know that every man who will read it prayerfully, every man who will desire to know whether it be of God or not has the promise, not of Joseph Smith or any living human being, but the promise of our Heavenly Father that they shall know of a surety that it is of God."[66]

David O. McKay (1873–1970). "[The Book of Mormon] is a physical fact, a sensible fact, there were witnesses to it, the reliability of those witnesses is established, there are monuments and memorials to it, and those monuments and memorials date back to the event itself." [67]

Joseph Fielding Smith (1876–1972). "I want to bear my testimony to you . . . that I know that the Book of Mormon is true; that Joseph Smith received it from the hand of God through an angel that was sent to reveal it, the same angel who, while living in this world, finished the

---

[64] Joseph F. Smith, "Divine Mission of Joseph Smith—Prediction and Promise Fulfilled—Many Others Will Yet Be Verified—The Worlds Hatred of the Saints—Indisputable Evidence of the Divine Origin of the Church—No Power Can Destroy It—The Effects of Obedience and Its Opposite," *Journal of Discourses*, 25:99–100.
[65] Heber J. Grant, in Conference Report, April 1929, 128–129.
[66] George Albert Smith, in Conference Report, April 1936, 15.
[67] *Gospel Ideals: Selections from the Discourses of David O. McKay: Ninth President of The Church of Jesus Christ of Latter-day Saints* (Salt Lake City: Improvement Era, 1953), 87.

record and sealed it up to come forth in this Dispensation of the Fulness of Times."[68]

Harold B. Lee (1899–1973). "By this second witness we may know more certainly the meaning of the teachings of the ancient prophets and, indeed, of the Master and His disciples as they lived and taught among men. This should inspire all who would be honest seekers after truth to put these two sacred scriptures together and study them as one book, understanding, as we do, their true relationship."[69]

Spencer W. Kimball (1895–1985). "[The Book of Mormon] is the word of God. It is a powerful second witness of Christ. . . . May you read it prayerfully, study it carefully, and receive for yourselves the testimony of its divinity."[70]

Ezra Taft Benson (1899–1994). "The Book of Mormon is the keystone in our witness of Jesus Christ, who is Himself the cornerstone of everything we do. It bears witness of His reality with power and clarity. Unlike the Bible, which passed through generations of copyists, translators, and corrupt religionists who tampered with the text, the Book of Mormon came from writer to reader in just one inspired step of translation. Therefore, its testimony of the Master is clear, undiluted, and full of power. . . . Truly, this divinely inspired book is a keystone in bearing witness to the world that Jesus is the Christ."[71]

Howard W. Hunter (1907–1995). "The Book of Mormon is the word of God. . . . It is the most remarkable volume in existence today. Read it carefully and prayerfully, and as you do, God will give you a testimony of its truthfulness as promised by Moroni."[72]

Gordon B. Hinckley (1910–2008). "For centuries the Bible stood alone as a written testimony of the divinity of Jesus of Nazareth. Now, at its side, stands a second and powerful witness which has come forth 'to the convincing of the Jew and Gentile that JESUS is the CHRIST, the ETERNAL GOD, manifesting himself unto all nations.'"[73]

---

[68] Joseph Fielding Smith, "The Book of Mormon, A Divine Record," *Improvement Era*, December 1961, 926.

[69] Harold B. Lee, *Ye Are the Light of the World* (Salt Lake City: Deseret Book, 1974), 91.

[70] Spencer W. Kimball, "The Book of Vital Messages," *Improvement Era*, June 1963, 493, 495.

[71] Ezra Taft Benson, "The Book of Mormon—Keystone of our Religion," *Ensign*, November 1986.

[72] Clyde J. Williams, *The Teachings of Howard W. Hunter* (Salt Lake City: Bookcraft, 1997), 54.

[73] Gordon B. Hinckley, "First Presidency Message: A Testimony Vibrant and True," *Ensign*, August 2005.

Thomas S. Monson (1927–2018). "The importance of having a firm and sure testimony of the Book of Mormon cannot be overstated. We live in a time of great trouble and wickedness. What will protect us from the sin and evil so prevalent in the world today? I maintain that a strong testimony of our Savior, Jesus Christ, and of His gospel will help see us through to safety."[74]

Russell M. Nelson (1924–). "The Book of Mormon is the centerpiece of the Restoration. It was written, preserved, and transmitted under the Lord's direction. It was translated 'by the gift and power of God.'"[75]

What you have learned thus far is that the Lord Himself testified of the truthfulness of the Book of Mormon (see D&C 20:8–10). The translator Joseph Smith knew it to be so (Articles of Faith 1:8). After being shown the golden plates by an angel, Three Witnesses—Oliver Cowdery, David Whitmer and Martin Harris—testified of the truthfulness of the Book of Mormon. Eight Witnesses were shown the plates by Joseph Smith and testified of the truthfulness of the Book of Mormon. Presidents of The Church of Jesus Christ of Latter-day Saints have testified that the Book of Mormon is the Word of God and Another Testament of Jesus Christ.

In humility, I testify to you also. I have read and studied the Book of Mormon. I have pondered, prayed, and fasted concerning its message. I have sought since my youth to know of its contents. Day after day, I have searched as an earnest inquirer after truth. I have found truth! I have discovered my greatest find, truly my pearl of great price. It is that the Book of Mormon writers wrote primarily about my Savior. They wrote of Him because of their conviction of His divinity, for they knew Him. Through their diligent efforts, I now know of Him. I testify that the Book of Mormon is a powerful, profound witness that Jesus is the Christ, the Son of the Eternal God. I am not alone in my testimony, for millions of Latter-day Saints and seekers of truth throughout the world so testify.

After all the written and spoken testimonies of the Book of Mormon, the key question is, what do *you* think of the book? As Elder Bruce R. McConkie masterfully said:

---

[74] Thomas S. Monson, "The Power of the Book of Mormon," *Ensign*, May 2017.
[75] Russell M. Nelson, "Catch the Wave," *Ensign*, May 2013 quoted in Kevin S. Hamilton, "The Converting Power of the Book of Mormon," *Ensign*, January 2016.

Either the Book of Mormon is true, or it is false; either it came from God, or it was spawned in the infernal realms. It declares plainly that all men must accept it as pure scripture or they will lose their souls. It is not and cannot be simply another treatise on religion; it either came from heaven or from hell. And it is time for all those who seek salvation to find out for themselves whether it is of the Lord or of Lucifer.[76]

If the book is what it claims to be, if the original record was written on plates of metal and revealed by an angel sent from God to Joseph Smith, if the translation was made by the power of God, then you have the right to know it is true. Consider for a moment asking God, the Eternal Father, in the name of His Son, Jesus Christ, if the Book of Mormon is what it is purported to be. I testify to you, "if ye shall ask with a sincere heart, with real intent, having faith in Christ, he will manifest the truth of it unto you, by the power of the Holy Ghost. And by the power of the Holy Ghost ye may know the truth of all things" (Moroni 10:4–5).

---

[76] Bruce R. McConkie, "What Think Ye of the Book of Mormon?" *Ensign*, November 1983.

ABOUT THE AUTHOR

DR. SUSAN EASTON BLACK JOINED the faculty of Brigham Young University in 1978 and taught Church history and doctrine until she retired to serve multiple missions with her husband, George Durrant. She is also past associate dean of general education and honors and director of Church history in the Religious Studies Center.

The recipient of numerous academic awards, she received the Karl G. Maeser Distinguished Faculty Lecturer Award in 2000, the highest award given a professor on the BYU Provo campus.

Susan has authored, edited, and compiled more than 100 books and more than 250 articles.